Taoist Astral Healing

Taoist Astral Healing

Chi Kung Healing Practices
Using Star and Planet Energies

Mantak Chia and Dirk Oellibrandt

Illustrations by Udon Jandee

Destiny Books

Rochester, Vermont

Destiny Books
One Park Street
Rochester, Vermont 05767
www.InnerTraditions.com

Destiny Books is a division of Inner Traditions International

Library of Congress Cataloging-in-Publication Data

Chia, Mantak, 1944–
Taoist astral healing : chi kung healing practices using star and
planet energies / Mantak Chia and Dirk Oellibrandt ;
illustrations: Udon Jandee.
p. cm.
Includes bibliographical references and index.
ISBN 0-89281-089-0
1. Qi gong. 2. Healing—Folklore. I. Title: Chi kung healing
principles using star and planet energies. II.
Oellibrandt, Dirk. III. Title.
RA781.8.C468 2004
613.7'1—dc22

2003023413

Printed and bound in China

10 9 8 7 6 5 4 3 2 1

Text design and layout by Priscilla Baker
This book was typeset in Janson with Present, Futura, and Diotima as
the display typefaces

Contents

Putting Taoist Astral Healing into Practice

The practices described in this book have been used successfully for thousands of years by Taoists trained by personal instruction. Readers should not undertake these practices without receiving personal instruction from a certified instructor of the Universal Tao System because some of these practices, if done improperly, may cause injury or result in health problems. This book is intended to supplement individual training with a Universal Tao instructor and to serve as a reference guide for these practices. Anyone who undertakes these practices on the basis of this book alone does so entirely at his or her own risk. Universal Tao instructors can be located at our websites:

www.universal-tao.com or www.taoinstructors.org

Taoist Cosmic Healing, which explores some of the theories and practices upon which this book is based, is available from Destiny Books at:

www.innertraditions.com

The meditations, practices, and techniques described herein are *not* intended to be used as an alternative or substitute for professional medical treatment and care. If a reader is suffering from a mental or emotional disorder, he or she should consult with an appropriate professional health care practitioner or therapist. Such problems should be corrected before one starts training.

This book does not attempt to give any medical diagnosis, treatment, prescription, or remedial recommendation in relation to any human disease, ailment, suffering, or physical condition whatsoever.

Chinese Medicine and Chi Kung emphasize balancing and strengthening the body so that it can heal itself. The meditations, internal exercises, and martial arts of the Universal Tao are basic approaches to this end. Follow the instructions for each exercise carefully, and do not neglect the foundations (such as the Microcosmic Orbit practice and any other supplemental exercises).

Also pay special attention to the warnings and suggestions. People who have high blood pressure, heart disease, or a generally weak condition should proceed cautiously, having received prior consent from a qualified medical practitioner. People with venereal disease should not attempt any practices involving sexual energy until they are free of the condition.

The Universal Tao and its staff and instructors cannot be responsible for the consequences of any practice or misuse of the information in this book. If the reader undertakes any exercise without strictly following the instructions, notes, and warnings, the responsibility must lie solely with the reader.

Acknowledgments

The Universal Tao Publications staff involved in the preparation and production of *Taoist Astral Healing* extends gratitude to the many generations of Taoist masters who have passed on their special lineage, in the form of an oral transmission, over thousands of years. We thank Taoist master I Yun (Yi Eng) for his openness in transmitting the formulas of Taoist Inner Alchemy.

We offer our eternal gratitude to our parents and teachers for their many gifts to us. Remembering them brings joy and satisfaction to our continued efforts in presenting the Universal Tao system. As always, their contribution has been crucial in presenting the concepts and techniques of the Universal Tao.

We wish to thank the thousands of unknown men and women of the Chinese healing arts who developed many of the methods and ideas presented in this book. We extend our gratitude to Master Lao Kang Wen for sharing his healing techniques.

We offer special thanks to Sarina Stone for her generous assistance in revising and editing the original edition of this book, and to illustrator Udon Jandee and photographer Saysunee Yongyod. Thanks to Juan Li for the use of his beautiful and visionary paintings illustrating Taoist esoteric practices. We also thank Susan Bridle and Vickie Trihy for their editorial expertise. In addition, we wish to thank Colin Campbell, Matt Gluck, Dennis Huntington, Annette Dirksen, and Dirk Gerd Al, for their writing and editorial contributions to the previous editions of this book.

We wish to further express our gratitude to all the instructors and students who have offered their time and advice to enhance this system, especially Felix Senn, Barry Spendlove, Chong-Mi Mueller, Clemens Kasa, Andrew Jan, Marga Vianu, Harald Roeder, Salvador March, Dr. Hans Leonhardy, Peter Kontaxakis, Thomas Hicklin, Gianni Dell'Orto, and Walter and Jutta Kellengerger.

We also wish to thank the scientists and testing institutes: Gerhard Eggelsberger, Institute for Applied Biocybernetics Feedback Research, Vienna, Austria; and Dr. Ronda Jessum, Biocybernetics Institute, San Diego, California.

EMPEROR FU HSI

Universal Tao and Cosmic Healing Chi Kung

INTRODUCTION

Taoism is a practice of studying and living the laws of the universe. It has its roots in a body of knowledge that many masters have gathered over thousands of years. The Cosmic Healing practice presented in this book is the fruit of deep meditation by highly advanced practitioners who lived an intimate relationship with the universe and nature, often in remote and isolated places.

A major role in the discovery of Taoism's practical way to work with the energy of the universe was played by the legendary Chinese emperor Fu Hsi, who has been credited in Chinese history with the discovery of the *pa kua*, the diagrammatic symbols that are the foundation of the *I Ching*, the most ancient Taoist book of wisdom. Historians of Chinese culture also credit Huang-Ti, the Yellow Emperor, for synthesizing Taoist practices in the domains of health and healing as well as the healing love practices more than five thousand years ago. He integrated a wealth of insights and practices from a wide variety of Taoist masters. This process of synthesis and accumulation of theory and practice continued to grow in subsequent millennia, until today. It is still evolving.

The theory and practices presented in this book build upon those explored in *Taoist Cosmic Healing* (see page ix) and are offered so that practitioners of this system of cultivating the body, the Chi, and the spirit may advance in their practice and development. *Chi* means "energy" or "life force"; *kung* means "work." Cosmic Healing Chi Kung is the cultivation of the ability to conduct Chi for the purposes of healing. We call this practice

"Cosmic Healing" because we ultimately learn to use the forces of nature, human will, and cosmic particles to transform negativity stored in the body. The Taoist recognizes that human beings have a limited capacity for Chi. However, if we are able to connect with the sources of Chi in the universe, we gain an infinite capacity for Chi, and we constantly fill ourselves with the unlimited abundance of energy around us. This book specifically focuses on the teachings of Taoist astrology, and explores how we can use this ancient wisdom about the energies of the cosmos in our spiritual and healing practice.

Taoist practice as we understand it is not religious in conventional terms, nor is it based on a creed or on transcendental principles. It is a practice of self-awareness and self-transformation through which we gradually become one with the cosmos. In this process we realize and actualize ourselves. Within the physical body, the soul body grows, and within the soul body, the spirit body evolves. It is in this process of subsequent energy transformations that we return to our origins and realize our original, intrinsic nature of which peace and freedom are the natural fruits.

There is a firm insistence in the Taoist wisdom tradition that any advance in energy transformation, or what in Western culture is called spiritual development, needs to be well rooted in the earth. Thus the initiation into the higher practices bears fruit, in the Taoist view, only to the extent that the practitioner is rooted and grounded. The terms *grounded* and *rooted* explain the need to establish stability both physically and mentally. A sick or mentally ill person cannot serve his or her community at the same level the healthy person does. Through this stability, Taoist practitioners may help themselves and others to lead fascinating lives and at the same time to grow spiritually by realizing their natural potential.

Essential to spiritual growth is that the Taoist practitioner cultivate a sense of purity, joyfulness in life, and a sense of wonder, thereby regaining and enhancing the openness and excitement of a small child. (Not surprisingly, the child stands in the Taoist tradition for purity and immortality.) In this way the practitioner develops his or her own sense of inner truth as a reflection of one's innate spiritual origin.

In the chapters that follow, we offer an approach to a transformative practice that integrates ancient Taoist insights with knowledge from several more contemporary sources, exploring a wide range of possibilities. We hope that the information presented in these chapters will help the reader to enhance his or her awareness, health, and quality of relationships, and thereby will also serve to improve the quality of society in general.

Knowledge of this material can also be used in personal healing and by those who help others to heal themselves. The powerful and positive results of this approach in thousands of treatments have encouraged us to share this information.

RECLAIMING HEAVEN AND EARTH

We propose that the reason for the generally poor quality of our lives and those of all of society is our distorted perception of who we are, where we originated, and what we are doing here on earth. At times, our lives do not reflect our full potential. Many centuries of conditioning by institutional religion and toxic living conditions have lowered our energy frequencies. Many believe that humankind is falling into a horizontal, materialistic culture in which sensitivity to our true origin has become obscured and in which we live cut off from the energies of heaven. As a result of repression and disconnection, we may be lost in guilt, project negative emotions onto others, and look for truth outside rather than within ourselves. This book is designed to help us reactivate the deep memory of who we are and enable us to live up to our full potential as human beings.

If this state of disconnection is further aggravated by unnatural ways of living, moving, and eating, spiritual malaise and materialist obsession may result. If we turn away from the higher intelligence of the universe, which is our only source of true knowing, we become like a space shuttle without a computer, communication, or navigation system, being run by a person with amnesia. We don't remember who we are, where we came from, or what we want to do.

When people live in an unawakened, half-numb state, unconscious of the ways in which they are caught in the past and afraid to look at themselves here and now, the conditions for health simply cannot exist. As this is the dominant state of social energy, it is not easy to avoid being trapped in it. Ungrounded people are resigned to this state, and if you ask them how they feel and how they are doing, they will tell you, "I'm doing okay." Their lives basically revolve around eating, sleeping, mating, security, and power. If they were to look deeply inside and were honest with themselves, they would most likely see that they are rather unhappy and feel empty inside. The deep fear of looking at this pain and emptiness prevents them from noticing that they have gravely suppressed their godly nature. The figure on page 4 illustrates how, when we are trapped in this condition of spiritual disconnection, we look

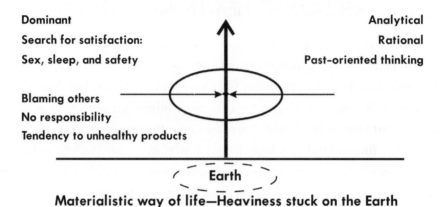

Horizontal Axis Dominant—Disconnecting from Heaven and Our Spiritual Source

Heaven

Religions / Scientific Conditioning / Unconscious Denial of Spiritual Origin

Dominant

Search for satisfaction:

Sex, sleep, and safety

Analytical

Rational

Past-oriented thinking

Blaming others

No responsibility

Tendency to unhealthy products

Earth

Materialistic way of life—Heaviness stuck on the Earth

HORIZONTAL AXIS DOMINANT

outside ourselves for satisfaction and security and use analytic thinking to repress our embodied experience.

Once we truly take responsibility for ourselves, our health, our spiritual origin, and our life task, we can start to wake up from this numb state. Then we become aware of the fear and mechanisms we have cultivated to prevent ourselves from getting in touch with our true selves. Only when we have the courage to look beneath the surface of our ordinary consciousness will we be able to open up and walk the path to freedom and spiritual independence.

As children of the universe, we are not only created by the divine intelligence and subtle substance of the cosmos, but if we allow it, we spontaneously will co-create its evolutionary process. We are not only children of the universe and its love that gave us life, we are also its fathers and mothers, whose love is co-responsible for the way it evolves. As an ancient expression says: "Embrace the universe as a mother embraces her firstborn child."

The "flower power" period and the New Age movement may be seen as a reaction to the materialistic upsurge. However, many followers of these movements, in their disdain of mundane and earthly material pursuits, have moved to the other extreme: a spirituality without grounding "roots" in the earth. In embracing spiritual ideals and rejecting material realities, they are trapped in the same duality between heaven and earth that has characterized most of history's dominant religious and philosophical traditions.

People with poor groundings and a negative relationship with their bodies frequently face a host of problems in their daily lives regarding sex, money, health, self-esteem, and relationships. They often suffer from insecurity and have an unhealthy relationship with the practical and emotional realities of their lives. They tend to seek ways to avoid or deny these realities, including their own physical existence, and thus experience a growing disconnection between body, mind, and spirit. They do understand that they need to look for truth within themselves, as they carry the divine within. But they find this difficult because of the split that they have created within themselves—between what is "above" and what is "below," between heaven and earth. The figure below illustrates this condition of physical disconnection, in which one tries to escape or transcend the complexities of embodied existence through using drugs or other avoidance techniques.

The pursuit of spiritual freedom often causes such aspirants to imprison themselves in their search. As a result they are bound to end up as imbalanced as their materialist opposites. It is the deep pain they experience that pushes them onto a spiritual path that they hope will be free from all worldly obstructions. Now the same ego is hidden behind a spiritual mask. When we turn our

Vertical Axis Dominant—Connection to Heaven and Spiritual Reality Disconnected from Earth and Physical Body

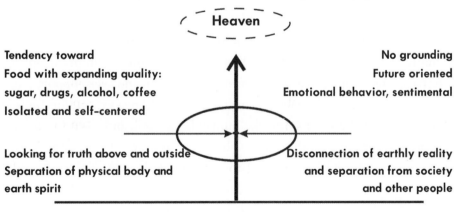

Physical Disconnection

VERTICAL AXIS DOMINANT

attention away from our body we cut the intelligence away from the "matter," and we dishonor the holiest temple on earth. The higher frequencies are not balanced and integrated in the physical body, so the vital essence will gradually leave the body or will transform into high energy frequencies that can only be partly assimilated in the physical body. Physically these individuals will start to slowly weaken and all kinds of symptoms will appear, ultimately leading to premature aging. Their heart-energy may be compared with a flower that is cut off from its roots; their spiritual condition is only momentary. They live only in the upper body, as they tend to ignore or are afraid of their sexuality, and they lack a connection with the belly, their energy center. And as love and sex are not connected, their relationships tend to be emotionally unstable and superficial.

Let us be true to ourselves: we were not given our bodies to deny them. Taoist self-healing practices can significantly help people in this condition of physical disconnection by teaching them how to get in touch with the true nature of their bodies, to care for them, and to make them healthy and strong. This is essential for the growth of a healthy energy body.

We can all contribute to the quality of life on this planet by dissolving the denseness and separation in our mind and our social mentality. The problem is not only in the body, but also in the absence and denial of an understanding of the infinite and unfathomable true spirit and universal mind. Taoist masters realize that truth lies in a spiritual life that includes the physical body. By consciously fusing the spirit with the core of physical existence, a new quality of life arises.

The initial focus of Taoist practice is creating a healthy and strong physical body, well rooted in the source of life, the energy of our "mother" earth. At the same time, Taoist practice acknowledges that the origin of our spirit is in heaven. Our soul has chosen to incarnate on earth and seeks opportunities to grow and evolve by learning from the universe. Since everything finds its nature in Tao or the great spirit, the human body, soul, and spirit can be seen as different densities of the same substance. In view of our unawakened, unconscious state, most of us tend to get trapped in one of the two poles, either by focusing on an earthly life at the expense of heaven or the other way around. The illustration opposite shows how, like a tree, healthy men and women are rooted both in the earth below and the universe above.

Over the ages, Taoist masters have obtained great understanding of the art of cultivating health and physical strength. Longevity was one of the fruits of their practice. In this way they enjoyed much time and space to cultivate

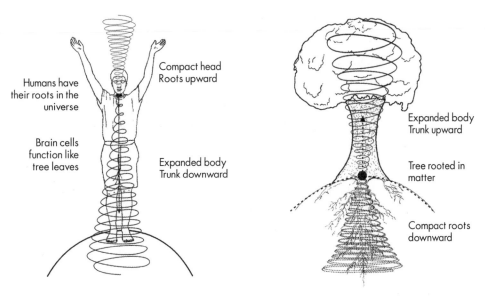

ROOTS OF HUMAN AND TREE

their knowledge and ability to conduct the various forms of Chi for self and planetary transformation.

With the deepening of the grounding practice, one's awareness grows step by step, and the emotions of daily life, with their ups and downs, gradually lose their uprooting effect. When one practices daily, one may reach a point where one feels the desire to withdraw from society and to live away from the hustle and bustle of modern life for a certain period of time in order to facilitate a truly intimate relationship with the universe and nature. This may speed up the transformation process, as has been demonstrated for centuries by monks within different spiritual traditions. However Taoist masters have also advised their students to give up their withdrawn lives and to return to "the world" to maintain their roots in the realities of daily life. This advice was given by a master if he observed that his students needed to mature or get a taste of social life and experience desire so that they could compare these two "directions" and appreciate the experience of true peace in their meditation practice. Additionally, before achieving a higher level of awareness and mastery over their energy, students were often sent for a few years into a busy town to work as dishwashers or do other menial jobs. Those students who reached the stage where they could maintain their inner peace, even under difficult circumstances, were seen as having become masters themselves.

For most people, withdrawal from society and from social relations and earthly life is only advisable after having learned and integrated several levels of energy transformation within society. If we withdraw from society without the necessary maturity and insight, the mind is bound to remain restless as it continues to look unceasingly for physical, emotional, and mental satisfaction.

When a Taoist student has achieved a strong navel center and enjoys a firm connection to heaven and earth within, he or she can freely move "upward" and "downward" without getting lost. (See the first volume of *Taoist Cosmic Healing* or *Chi Nei Tsang, Chinese Abdominal Chi Massage*, by Mantak Chia, for teachings about the navel center.) The relationship between heaven and earth may be represented by a vertical axis that goes up (heaven) and moves down (earth). Along this axis we can visualize the different centers and levels of energy and their transformations (body/soul/spirit). Because of its tradition of firm rooting, the Taoist way of energy transformation is a safe one. It has been tested for many centuries. The Universal Tao practice is a self-cultivation program that we can use and apply effectively in our daily lives. The practices lead us step by step from an initial level to the highest or "immortal" practices. The Taoist way of life teaches us to reconnect with and become aware of our true spiritual origin and bring this experience down into the lowest center of the physical body, the lower Tan Tien (see page 12). It brings spirit into matter or light to earth. The figure below illustrates how, after achieving this strong rooting process between heaven and earth (vertical axis), practitioners can move freely into the materialistic world (horizontal axis) without losing their connection with the spiritual.

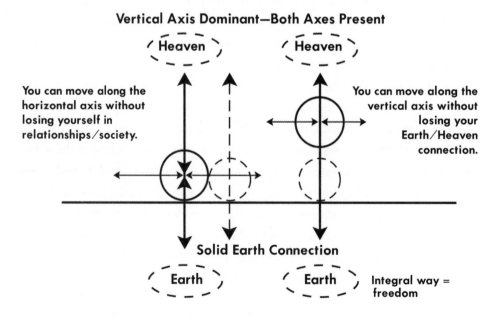

TAOIST WAY: BALANCE BETWEEN VERTICAL AND HORIZONTAL AXES

THREE SOURCES OF CHI

The subtle origin of the universe and the Tao is the source of all life, all beings, all things, all energy, and all their various manifestations. In the Tai Chi symbol (below, center), the circle represents the oneness and the yin and yang energies represent the intrinsic polarity of all forms of energy. Yin and yang represent a unity of opposites, always balancing, completing, embracing, and containing each other.

According to the Taoist view, the energy of the universe is comprised of three different realms. The interaction between yin and yang created the "three pure ones" or the three energy sources in the universe: the cosmic force, the universal force, and the earth force. Knowing that these energies contain the pure light of the Tao, we recognize the three pure ones in the three interlocking circles of the triple unity symbol (below, right). The circle of the Tai Chi symbol can also be understood to represent the cosmic light energy while yang and yin represent the universal and the earth energy.

Oneness Unity   **Yin/Yang Tai Chi**   **Triple Unity—Cosmic** **—Universal** **—Earth** ⎱ **Chi**

TAO OF TRIPLE UNITY

Cosmic Chi is born out of the original Chi of the Tao and literally carries the intelligence and essence of life. Guided by this intelligence, it spreads out into the universe and manifests in different densities and forms defined by the cosmic laws. This is how stars, planets, human cells, subatomic particles, and all other forms of life take form and are nourished.

In particular, cosmic energy descends and materializes into the human baby as it is attracted into the world by the magnetic field between the earth and the moon. Since most people have lost the ability to consciously and directly absorb the cosmic light, we can only do this in a materialized form, either by eating living substances that have absorbed cosmic light (plants) or by eating living creatures (animals) that have eaten the plants. This means that we only consume light in a more or less materialized form: cosmic dust, which in turn becomes plants and animals. Evolution is leading us to once again be able to consume from the source: cosmic light. In this way yin and yang have become each other, as the circle leads us back into light after so many years of disconnection from the source.

Taoist practice focuses on restoring this direct connection with the cosmic source (light particles) so that we regain the ability to directly live from light energy. As we develop this capacity, we become less and less dependent on eating plants and animals. Taoist legends tell us that throughout the ages, some Taoist masters have been able to live for months or even years without taking any food and without losing weight, while maintaining and even enhancing their vitality. Today, there are reports that a number of people from different backgrounds throughout the world are living only on water, tea, or fruit juice. This practice may be possible because such advanced practitioners tap into cosmic light, the original source of human life and all other forms of being.

Universal and earth energy, or Chi, also have their genesis in the original energy of the Tao. The universal Chi is the radiating force of all galaxies, stars, and planets throughout the whole universe. It is the all-pervasive force that nourishes the life energy in all the forms of nature. The earth force is the third force of nature, which includes all the energies of mother earth. This force is activated by the electromagnetic field originating in the rotation of the earth. It is also integrated into all aspects of nature on our planet. The earth energy is accessed through the soles of the feet, the perineum, and the sexual organs. Earth energy nourishes the physical body. It supplies our daily life force and is one of the principal forces used to heal ourselves.

HUMAN ENERGY IN THE UNIVERSE

In early times Taoist masters had an understanding of what a human being truly *is* that is quite different from many present-day theories. Human energy was understood to be the highest manifestation of cosmic light. The primary responsibility of humankind, as this highest manifestation of cosmic light, was seen to be keeping the balance between heaven and earth. This balance between heaven and earths parallels the balance between humankind and earth; it was understood that, as intelligent creatures, we have responsibility for maintaining peace and harmony on the planet so that we may have a safe space to evolve. Today, this responsibility is frequently experienced as a bur-

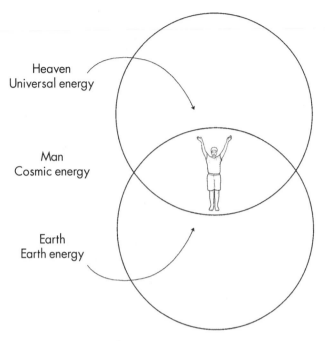

Heaven
Universal energy

Man
Cosmic energy

Earth
Earth energy

<small>BALANCE BETWEEN HEAVEN AND EARTH</small>

den and not as an opportunity to grow. Yet each of us holds the memory, within our genetic code, of our true potential and of our true role and responsibility as human beings.

THE THREE LEVELS OF EXISTENCE AND THE THREE TAN TIENS

The threefold nature of the universe manifests itself in many different ways. In the Taoist vision, everything we see and experience around us has gone through three different realms or spheres of existence.

The subtle origin is the source of everything, heaven and earth. It contains the realm of Chi and all phenomena.

1. The subtle origin or pure law of existence (Tao).
2. Chi, the subtle energy.
3. All phenomena, interactions, and transformations of Chi.

The three realms are inseparable. Once we understand this threefold nature and experience its manifestation in our bodies, we have made a major step on our spiritual journey.

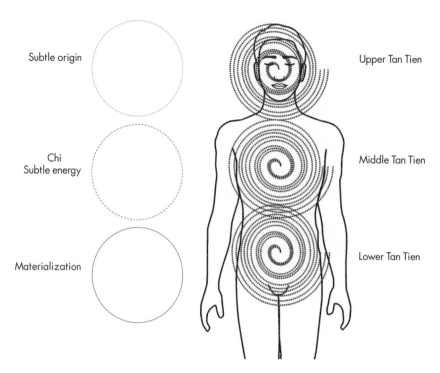

Subtle origin

Chi
Subtle energy

Materialization

Upper Tan Tien

Middle Tan Tien

Lower Tan Tien

THE THREE TAN TIENS IN THE HUMAN BODY

We have pointed to the necessity of opening up the vertical axis and establishing a deep rooting in both heaven and earth. The three principal energy centers in our body on this axis are called *Tan Tiens*. They are in reality the containers of the physical, soul, and spirit energy. The way we become human is through a process of materialization (the body is the material densification of energy) in which the subtle energy of the Tao, connected to your spirit, incarnates through your soul into your body. Heaven descends into the earth, and what is above and below are united. The three Tan Tiens (above) each have specific energetic functions. The three main stages in Taoist spiritual cultivation are directly related to the three Tan Tiens.

The lower energy center, or Tan Tien, also called the "lower fire," is located behind and below the navel. It is found in the triangle between the navel, the "kidney center point" (in the spine between the second and third lumbar, also called the "gate of life"), and the sexual center. For men, the sexual center is the prostate gland and for women it lies in the top of the cervix between the ovaries.

The lower Tan Tien has a strong polarity because it governs the fire element in the small intestine and the sexual and kidney energy (water) at the same time. It is the center of the physical body and of physical strength. It

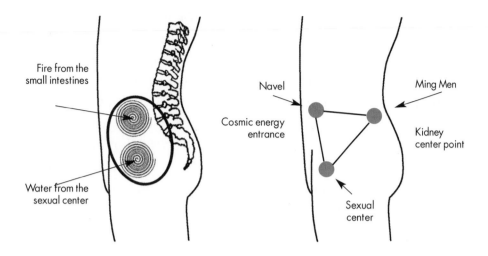

LOCATION OF THE LOWER TAN TIEN WITHIN THE TRIANGLE

contains a frequency of gross energy (compared to the more subtle energies of the two other Tan Tiens). When the lower Tan Tien is strong, digestion is easy, emotions and experiences are easily transformed, and there is much sexual energy.

The lower Tan Tien contains the basic spark that was created when your father's sperm penetrated your mother's egg. If this spark continues to be active and strong, it provides life force to the billions of cells throughout your body. Control of sexual energy and its transformation into life force is essential if we wish to raise our energy level in the lower Tan Tien. For men this implies preserving the life essence of the sperm during intercourse or self-stimulation. Through controlling ejaculation they can transform the essence of the sperm into Chi. For women it means learning to regulate and control menstruation, thereby transforming blood into Chi. The practices for cultivating the ability to control and transform sexual energy are presented in the first two chapters of *Taoist Cosmic Healing*, by Mantak Chia. For healers, it is very important to learn how to transform sexual energy into spiritual energy. The original balance between love and sex, or water and fire, contains in itself the essence of healing and creation. Self-transformation is a precondition for being able to help others on the path of transforming sexual energy into spiritual energy.

Another vital transformation that occurs within the lower Tan Tien is the transformation of negative emotions. (A thorough explanation of this process may be found in the books *Healing Love* and *Cultivating Male or Female Sexual Energy* by Mantak Chia.)

Once the energy in the lower Tan Tien has become pure and strong through the transformation of sexual energy and negative emotions, it will naturally ascend to the heart center, the middle Tan Tien. In this way, a purer, higher-frequency energy arises and radiates from the heart. True compassion and love, as a higher energy state, are the fruit of the transformation of the energies of the organs. This compassion is developed by cultivating positive virtues and by good deeds, and is stored in the soul body. True compassion should not be mistaken for the dualistic, sentimental love that all of us have experienced temporarily during peak love experiences at times in our life.

The true, godly nature of our being and our love starts radiating through our higher-self connection in and from the middle Tan Tien, our heart center. In this state there is an abundance of energy, as the heart center is directly nourished by the cosmic light, and we experience a deep oneness with people around us. This higher energy and awareness level allows us to help others while not losing energy ourselves. The light of compassion that is born from universal love can be cultivated and will gradually attract more pure divine light and spiritual essence.

This spiritual essence is then attracted by the upper Tan Tien, and experienced practitioners will guide the energy to specific ends, depending on the particular practice they are performing. The upper Tan Tien is composed of the glands in the crown of the head at the core of the nervous system, and, indeed, is the whole of one's crown. It is seen as a compact, spiral-shaped center that gathers the spiritual essence and transmutes it into a "crystal body," a body that does not dissolve at the moment of death and that carries us to immortality. The center of the crown is known as the "crystal palace." The pituitary gland is located in the crown and its location in the brain directly corresponds to the "crystal palace" point. This gland, when properly activated, will assist with hormonal and glandular functions. The highest levels of refinement of energy happen in the upper Tan Tien.

In this process—whereby Chi is strengthened, purified, and transformed through the three "cauldrons" of the Tan Tiens—the nature of our life changes and adopts a divine quality. The actions and directions we choose come from the laws of the universe and are no longer determined by animalistic behavior, emotional satisfaction, or a drive for wealth and power. It is a lifelong process of self-cultivation that gradually takes us from the suffering of addiction and dependence and the ups and downs of extreme emotions to a life of freedom, spiritual independence, and enlightenment.

This process of transformation facilitates the cultivation of the three bodies illustrated at right and leads to:

- a healthy body and an abundance of life force;
- control and balance on the emotional level and the growth of the compassionate heart center;
- the maturation of the soul body, which then nurtures the spirit body;
- the uniting of body, soul, and spirit deep within the three Tan Tiens, enlightening the person;
- the ability to share this light and wisdom with everybody around one.

When the three bodies are established and spiritual energy is dictating the quality of life, the practitioner can transform energy from the physical into the soul body and from the soul into the spirit body.

Since the soul carries the seed of the immortal or spirit body within, the development of the spirit body is the prerequisite for breaking through the law and the wheel of incarnation. In the higher levels of Taoist practice, one actualizes all of the soul's lessons and forgoes the necessity to reincarnate in order to grow as a spiritual being. This, combined with the ability to control all forms of Chi, enables the practitioner to choose to take his or her body into the next realm. At the moment of death, the energy of the physical body is partly or completely absorbed into the spirit body. When this energy is absorbed into the spirit body, the physical body eventually dissolves. There are many legends of Taoist masters who successfully dissolved their physical body rapidly into the spirit body, leaving only teeth, hair, and nails.

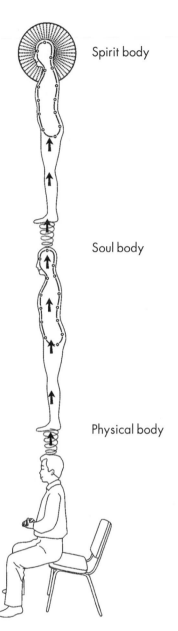

Spirit body

Soul body

Physical body

THREE BODIES

UNIVERSAL TAO BASIC PRACTICES AND PREPARATION EXERCISES

In the Universal Tao System, we teach Cosmic Healing Chi Kung within a comprehensive framework of exercises and meditation. As a part of this system, Cosmic Healing addresses the art of healing oneself and others, and

Universal Tao and Cosmic Healing Chi Kung

focuses on cultivating the ability to sense, control, strengthen, and project Chi. One can easily learn the simple exercises of Cosmic Healing Chi Kung without doing any other Universal Tao practices, but if one truly wishes to master the art of Cosmic Healing, it is important to have a firm foundation in the basic Universal Tao practices. Therefore we suggest that you become familiar with the basic practices and exercises outlined in the first three chapters of *Taoist Cosmic Healing* before proceeding with the advanced theory and techniques discussed in the following chapters. Throughout this book, we will refer periodically to these preparatory practices and will direct you to *Taoist Cosmic Healing* (see page ix).

Taoist Astrology and the Structure of the Universe

THE ORIGINS OF TAOIST ASTROLOGY

Thousands of years ago, people experienced the shimmering stars as their natural connection with heaven. Society was organized in accordance with the laws of the universe, and people viewed their relations as a reflection of the configurations of the stars. Human arrogance, the drive for power, and a growing disdain for nature led to the vision that the earth was the center of the universe rather than our temporary home and central point from which to observe the universe. Leaders began to rule their countries without being in touch with the heavens. A mixture of power, ambition, desire for wealth, and religious conditioning led to an increasing disconnection from the natural receptivity to the energy of the universe.

Since then, this self-created isolation has been growing and is dominant in present-day society. While there is a longing to reconnect, and while many healers, therapists, and practitioners of meditation or astrology understand the ancient practices with their rational minds, they often miss the subtle connections.

The knowledge with which astrologists now work originated in the direct experiential connection with and deep understanding of the universe that many masters cultivated throughout several thousand years. Many people wonder how the early astrologists, who wrote down their experiences and transmitted their knowledge to future generations, gathered their information, for they had no telescopes or sophisticated equipment. Through a combination of intimately observing the universe and relating these observations to changes in the energy on earth, in nature, and in human beings, as well as through meditation and spiritual practices, the Taoist master astrologers were able to assemble their knowledge.

During the Tang dynasty (618–907 C.E.) many Taoist masters and students spent their whole lives in *kuans,* or observatories. The masters selected unique locations in nature for the *kuans,* based on the presence of strong cosmic energy. Most of the *kuans* were located high in the mountains, sometimes in very inaccessible places. The interaction of strong natural forces with the natural "crystal antennas" of the mountains, along with the planetary/star observations and meditations in which they engaged, formed a perfect platform for the Taoist astral travel and spiritual practices.

These masters clearly saw the cranium as our own bony planetarium. A key discovery was breaking through the illusion of the separateness of "inner" and "outer." Their supernatural astrology helped them to realize the universe within the cranium, and from there, to channel the universal energies into the three Tan Tiens. In the Taoist view, these highly advanced insights could only come about through the growth of the higher centers and glands, which allowed them to perceive and understand the reality of the universe beyond the normal material and visible manifestations. Taoists say, "Without leaving the room, you can know heaven and earth."

Of course, modern astronomy provides us with a great deal of interesting information. We should realize that our understanding of universal laws can be further enhanced by the discoveries of modern astrophysics.

Yet the Newtonian view of the universe, which has dominated modern science and thought for the past several centuries, uses a mechanical approach to reality. Its exclusively rational methodology, which ignores our bodies and our ability to sense and use our intuition and feelings, has gradually and increasingly disconnected us from the realm of the spirit and the living cosmos. Strangely enough, the more we attempted to know the universe through observation with a telescope, the more we became separated from its subtle origin.

Because the rational mind tends to move horizontally, it finds it difficult to enter into the realm of the spiritual laws (unless, of course, it is the rational mind of a spiritually evolved person). Each time an astronomer reaches further into the universe, finding new information, scientists try to use this information to form a new concept about the history and origin of the cosmos. But these fundamental questions cannot be answered within the realm of time and space. It is good news that a growing number of modern scien-

ASTROLOGER CASTING A HOROSCOPE

tists are becoming more open to a new (yet ancient) paradigm that views the universe as having a timeless and spaceless origin. And many scientists who previously subscribed to the Newtonian view now agree that the essence of the material world is energy waves that appear as matter to the external senses. Some scientists, however, believe that by the year 2030, the computer will be able to take over the complete function of the human brain. This idea shows a very limited understanding of the true nature of our intelligence and the human mind.

"As above, so below": We tend to look at ourselves in the same way that we look at the universe, even if we are not conscious of the direct connection between the two. While the insights of modern science—from macrocosmic astronomy to microscopic biology—may expand our understanding of the universe, it is the direct, intimate connection with the universe and our bodies that provides the deep knowledge that illuminates our spiritual practice. It is this knowledge that the ancient Taoist astrologers cultivated, and that we can utilize today. What makes the Cosmic Healing Chi Kung practice so powerful is that the more we practice connecting to this vast resource we call "the universe," the more we are able to conduct this energy for the purpose of health and healing.

ASTROLOGY IS INFLUENCE, NOT DESTINY

Ancient peoples believed that the specific conditions, locations, and relationships of stars and planets at the moment of birth largely determined the personality and tendencies of the human being and the influences by which his or her life are patterned. As we study and utilize the insights of astrology, it is important to see astrological influences as strong tendencies and not as a fatalistic prediction or inevitable destiny. The unique qualities of our astrological makeup will indeed influence us for the rest of our lives. But it is important to see that these conditions work on our body and soul, not on our spirit. Taoists believe that the reason for this is that the spirit is eternal. It has always existed, and will always exist. It is free from the laws of karma and reincarnation. It is therefore free from the laws governing individual incarnations. For that reason Taoist astrologists say that astrological conditions should not be seen as limitations but rather as directions based on universal influences.

Astrology gives us clear information about where we come from and how our tendencies may evolve. Since our spirit is timeless and spaceless, we can still move in any direction. An intelligent person moves with the flow and intelligence of the universe in order to sustain the life force inside. It is good to remember that we can move in the direction in which we truly wish to move, always following the truth within our hearts. If we decide to join a football game, we are immediately fixed by the rules of the game. If we see all these rules as limitations, we would do better to play another game. The art of playing the game of life is to see, understand, and accept the limits in the material world and learn how to move freely within them, while maintaining awareness of our connection with our unlimited spirit.

Two basic questions to ask when making a major life choice or choosing a new direction are: "Where am I now?" and "What is the best way to achieve my goal?" Through the connection with our spiritual origin and the planetary/galactic forces, we can strengthen the weaker points in our energy system and our personality. In this way we can use astrological information as a source of personal growth and not as an excuse for unconscious or emotional behavior.

A BRIEF HISTORY OF ASTROLOGY

Chinese astrology is a very broad subject that contains an enormous amount of information and that may seem highly complicated for the untrained mind. There are many ways of interpreting the universal conditions, which are brought together in different systems with their own specific diagrams and calculation methods.

In ancient Taoist literature much attention is given to the subject of astrology. The eighteenth-century Chinese Imperial Encyclopedia has 2,500 chapters on astrology! What we wish to do in this book is to make you aware of the nature and origin of this wisdom and how it relates to spiritual practices and the laws of the universe.

In most Chinese astrological systems it is asserted that between four and five thousand years ago, the stars and planets were perfectly situated. While it is difficult to describe what this means from a pragmatic point of view, it is clear that this period was seen as a unique condition in the cosmos. From that point on, Chinese astrologers have counted the years, months, and days and calculated stellar and planetary movements by observing the sky. Noio, the Great Minister of the Yellow Emperor Huang-Ti, set the beginning of the Chinese calendar and its first sixty-year cycle at 2637 B.C.E. According to the Chinese calendar, we are in the seventy-eighth sexagesimal (sixty-year) cycle now. Each year of the sexagesimal cycle is given a name that is made up of two parts, the "heavenly stem" and the "earthly branch."

Most sources claim that Chinese astrology developed wholly independently from other cultures and traditions, but this is probably not the case. If we compare Chinese, Mayan, and old European calendars and zodiacs, as well as their language and architecture, we find parallels that simply cannot be accidental. It is clear that all these cultures were shaped by the same information source. The advanced spiritual development of these different cultures allowed them to translate this information into astrological systems that reflected the order of the universe. This translation happened in coordination with their specific locations on the planet.

Ancient civilizations all over the world were already observing the stars long before the start of the Chinese calendar in 2637 B.C.E. Archaeological findings from the ancient cultures of Egypt, Sumeria, Babylon, India, Greece, and Peru indicate that these peoples observed the movements and laws of the heavens. For example, although there is still debate on the subject, the renowned Egyptologist R. A. Schwaller de Lubicz states that the starting point of the Egyptian calendar is approximately 4240 B.C.E. This calendar was based on astronomical observations made during a period more than six thousand years ago. In ancient Egyptian civilization, astronomy/astrology was used to gain knowledge about universal laws, which was then codified into laws and principles for governing human life. The Great Pyramid of Khufu was built in approximately 2500 B.C.E. One of its functions was to serve as an astronomical observatory. The entire geometry of the pyramid was based upon calculations of astronomical positions and movements.

DIFFERENCES BETWEEN CHINESE AND WESTERN ASTROLOGY

The main differences between Chinese and Western astrology are their reference points. In Western astrology, stellar positions are calculated in reference to the plane of the ecliptic, which is the plane defined by the trajectory the sun apparently makes around the earth. The plane of the ecliptic is

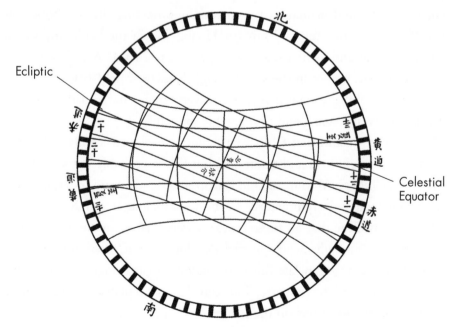

Ecliptic

Celestial Equator

THE RED ROUTE (CELESTIAL EQUATOR) AND YELLOW ROUTE (ECLIPTIC)

inclined at an angle of twenty-three degrees from the plane of the equator. The ecliptic is also used in Chinese astrology, and is known as the "yellow route," but the North Star is seen as the central reference point in the sky. Several thousand years ago, Taoist masters observed that the North Star always keeps its position while the twenty-eight constellations turn around it. For this reason Taoists have always seen the North Star as the center of the star world and also as the gate to the spiritual realm and the Tao. Therefore the celestial equator (the "red route"), which is the projection of the earth's equator onto the sky, is seen as the baseline.

In this context, Chinese astrology uses a lunar zodiac that references the moon's cycle around the earth (twenty-eight days) and that divides each day into twenty-eight segments. This is also related with the twenty-eight years it takes Saturn to orbit the sun.

The Chinese zodiac, or twelve-animal cycle, also refers to the twelve years it takes planet Jupiter to orbit the sun. The animal names used in Chinese astrology came to China from India. According to legend, the Buddha was visited by twelve animals that came to say good-bye to him before he left the earth.

The Chinese calendar is based on sexagesimal cycles, with the years and days marked by a system that combines "heavenly stems" and "earthly branches." There are ten heavenly stems, which refer to the five elements

WESTERN ZODIAC, ZODIAC BAND, AND PLANE OF THE ECLIPTIC
The solar zodiac band extends above and below the plane of the ecliptic.
Zodiacs with twelve signs are known in many different cultures.

(water, metal, earth, fire, and wood), each of which has a yin and a yang mode. The earthly branches are twelve in number and refer to the twelve animals.

The strongest difference between modern Western and traditional Chinese astrology is the focus on the North Star as the "heavenly gate." (Taoist Cosmic Healing Chi Kung derives very special and powerful healing energy from the North Star.) There has always been a direct relationship between Chinese astrology and the Taoist spiritual practices, and Chinese astrology has always been linked to direct astronomical observation. Chinese astrologers made observations constantly and based many of their calculations directly upon them. The movement and appearance of planets and stars, including their brightness, aura, and shades, were closely studied. Some Chinese emperors had twenty-four-hour observation crews. In this way, all signs from the universe were picked up and used to make personal and political decisions. Many stars and planets were connected to gods, emperors, or sages. Changes in the expressions of heavenly bodies were seen as direct signs from the divine world. Although they had no astronomical tools, Taoist astronomers knew about supernovae (exploding stars), black holes (imploding stars), pulsars, and quasars.

As we have noted, Chinese astrology is based on direct observation of the sky, and it is used in this book as a means of understanding and working with universal energy. Many astrologers all over the world now focus solely on their charts and books, only looking down rather than connecting with the universe. Even in China, the traditional art of astrology is hard to find these days. It has been taken over by Western astrology or other methods of prediction. Very few practitioners still combine their astrological calculations with spiritual practice and close observation of the sky.

Although much more of ancient China's knowledge and information has been recorded and preserved than has been the case with other ancient civilizations, the real meaning of many of its methods and systems of knowledge is rarely ascertained. The system of heavenly stems and earthly branches is a good example of this. Today this system is used on computers and in the form of diagrams by many practitioners of Chinese medicine all over the world, but very few of them know what the system really means and where it comes from.

CHINESE ZODIAC

HINDU ZODIAC

CHINESE ASTROLOGY AND THE LAWS OF THE UNIVERSE

As human beings, we are the highest manifestation of the cosmic light, which has its origin directly in the Tao, the oneness. The life we lead originates from this source. From this one, unlimited intelligence a process of densification, materialization, and multiplication has led to our individual incarnation or manifestation in the physical realm. Taoist philosophy describes this process as "the one giving birth to the two." The interaction between the two results in the differentiation and multiplicity of the world of phenomena. To connect to the spiritualizing spiral of true intelligence that we are will strengthen the connection to the Tao. In other words, the more we understand nature and the universe, the more we understand ourselves. We can deepen this process through astronomical observation and meditation, which is discussed later in this book.

As we discussed earlier, in Chinese cosmology and philosophy, the world of duality, of yin and yang, gives birth to the triple unity. This triple unity we find in the three basic energies in the universe (cosmic, universal, and earth energies) and in the interaction between human, heaven, and earth. In the human body, the interaction of heaven and earth forces (two) gives birth to the three Tan Tiens.

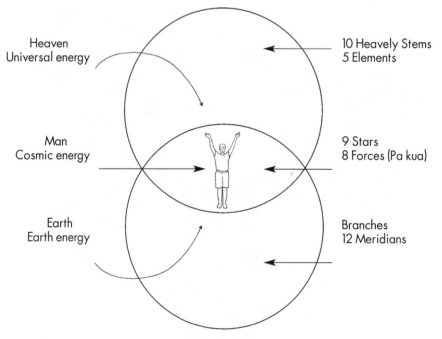

INTERACTION OF MAN WITH THE REALMS OF HEAVEN AND EARTH, THE PA KUA AND THE STEMS AND BRANCHES

The principles of Chinese philosophy and astrology apply to the cosmic, universal, and earth realms in a number of complex and interrelated ways. The ten heavenly stems are based on the yin and yang aspects of the five elements, which we will explore in more detail a little later.

The eight trigrams, or *pa kua*, of the *I Ching* correspond to the "eight forces" and the "eight extraordinary meridians" in the body. In Chinese medicine there are eight forces of nature that correspond to various organs and that rule the body. Meridians are channels in the body through which energy passes. The eight extraordinary meridians are among the most important energy pathways. This meridian system is nurtured by the eight planets and the eight related star essences.

The principles of the *pa kua* are also found in the Taoist "nine-star astrology" system, which incorporates the eight forces with the central Tai Chi (a symbol in which the yin/yang is surrounded by the *pa kua* trigrams) to make nine stars.

The North Star and Big Dipper energy are particularly important in the Taoist Cosmic Healing practice. Taoist masters observed that nine major energy points clearly reflect the changing energy qualities of the universe and our planet. These nine points are the seven stars of the Big Dipper, Polaris (the North Star), and Vega.

The twelve earthly branches, which correspond to the twelve animals of the Chinese zodiac, are in relationship with the earthly forces and also the twelve main acupuncture channels.

The ten heavenly stems have a high-frequency energy, and are related both to cosmic law and to universal energy. The twelve earthly branches have a lower frequency and are related to the earth energy and the surroundings of the earth in the twelve different directions.

The principles of the five elements, the *pa kua* trigrams, and, to a lesser degree, the related stems and branches, are fundamental to the planetary and stellar meditations of Cosmic Healing Chi Kung. We will go deeper into these topics as we progress.

The Five Elements

The law of yin and yang, the five elements, the eight forces, and the eight trigrams of the *pa kua* come from the unmanifested world and control the whole world of phenomena, including the world of stars and planets and life on earth. Every part of Chinese philosophy is connected with the five elements.

Written evidence of the use of the five elements dates back to around 300 B.C.E., although they were certainly known and used before that time. Much confusion arises between the Greek four elements (water, air, earth, and fire) and the Chinese five elements (wood, fire, earth, metal, and water). Both systems have a clear underlying philosophy. In the Chinese system, the five basic planets (Mars, Saturn, Venus, Mercury, Jupiter) are seen as the physical manifestation of the five elements.

Ancient Chinese astrology divides the sky into five "palaces." The region directly above the North Pole is the "central palace," which is visible throughout the year. The other four palaces can be located as the earth moves through the four seasons during its annual rotation around the sun. Each of the outer four palaces covers an area of about ninety degrees in the sky.

The one (circle) gives birth to the two (yin and yang), and from there we find the three (for example, heaven, earth, and man). A further differentiation leads us to the *pa kua*. Inside the eight *pa kua* trigrams, we find the five elements: earth, fire, metal, water, and wood (see illustrations opposite). The various combinations of the eight principal trigrams gives us the sixty-four trigrams used in the *I Ching*. An understanding of these concepts about the order of the universe and its governing laws was traditionally necessary to be able to work with Chinese astrology.

The relationship between the *pa kua* trigrams and the five directions and five elements can be looked at in a number of different ways. In a common manner of visualizing them, the five elements are located as follows within an octagonal form: earth as the center, south on top, north below, east left, west right. If the observers look to the south, they see the chart as shown below left.

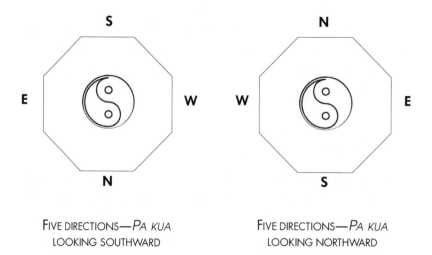

FIVE DIRECTIONS—*PA KUA*
LOOKING SOUTHWARD

FIVE DIRECTIONS—*PA KUA*
LOOKING NORTHWARD

But if we look northward, then north would be on top, south bottom, east right, west left. The illustration on the right at the bottom of the opposite page shows the diagram from the perspective of a north-facing observer.

It has been a tradition in Universal Tao teachings to be aware of both points of view.

A common way of working with the five elements is to relate each element to a season (adding a fifth season, Indian summer). The earth element corresponds to Indian summer; this follows the fire element, which corresponds to summer; the wood element corresponds to spring, and so on (see first diagram below). Another less popular method places the earth in the center as well as in short earth periods between every season (bottom diagram).

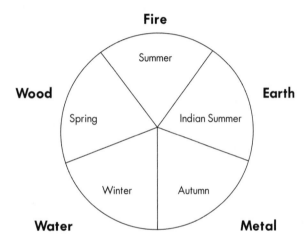

MOST COMMON WAY OF USING THE FIVE ELEMENTS IN THE YEAR'S CYCLE
There are five periods of 72 days each (within a 360-day astrological year).

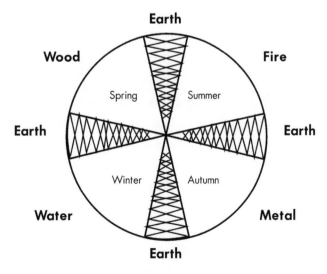

ANOTHER WAY TO VIEW THE ELEMENTS IN THE YEAR'S CYCLE
The earth element is seen as the changing and balancing point between the seasons.

The dominance of one of the five elements in a person's basic energy will give a specific character or charge to the person's quality and way of living. Of course, all of us have some of all five elements within our astrological makeup, but according to the year, month, and day of our birth, and in some systems also the hour and minute of our birth, one of the five elements will be stronger than the other four. Many books and websites provide instruction for determining your own predominant element and astrological influences. As we mentioned before, there are many different systems, all using different methods to make calculations. Most of them work well if we understand their point of view and if we use them as a "whole." Mixing different astrological systems tends to create much confusion.

The most typical positive or creative qualities of the different elements are:

Wood: Practical, creative, casual
Fire: Lively, talkative, quick
Earth: Stable, reliable, conservative, primitive
Metal: Vigorous, progressive, determined, calculated
Water: Contemplative, attentive, communicative, adjustable

(For a better understanding of this topic, see *Fusion of the Five Elements 1* by Mantak Chia.)

The *Pa kua* and Eight Forces

The eight trigrams of the *pa kua* were first described by the legendary emperor Fu Hsi as a sign from heaven brought in the form of stripes on the back of a turtle. The *I Ching*, or "Book of Changes," is based on these trigrams. The combinations of the trigrams give birth to the sixty-four hexagrams used in the *I Ching* and in *I Ching* astrology. The eight trigrams are also known as the "eight forces" and the "eight directions."

In Chinese medicine there are often three or four names for one thing or idea. Furthermore, one term may have multiple meanings. For example, the trigram *Kan* has a number of meanings, including: north, water, winter, kidney, and Mercury. It is the nature of Chinese symbols to explain many things with one term.

The heavens are divided into numerous regions, called *palaces*, which refer to areas of the heavens demarcated by the projection of the different directions and the center (the North Pole) into the sky. Chinese astrology sometimes refers to five palaces (the four directions and the center), and at other times to nine (the eight directions and the center). Nine palaces are used in the *Chiu Kung Ming Li,* or "nine-star astrology." The *pa kua* trigrams are also used in the Lo Pan, the basic tool of Chinese divination and geomancy (see below), and in Feng Shui, the art of creating harmonious environments.

The eight trigrams come from the combinations between the yin ▬ ▬ and the yang ▬▬▬ .

First there was the Grand One ▬▬▬▬▬▬▬▬ ; this produced the two poles yin ▬ ▬ and yang ▬▬▬▬ ; the two poles yielded four phases, the four strengths: greater yang *(tai yang)*, lesser yang *(shao yang)*, greater yin *(tai yin)*, and lesser yin *(shao yin)*. The four phases yield the eight trigrams.

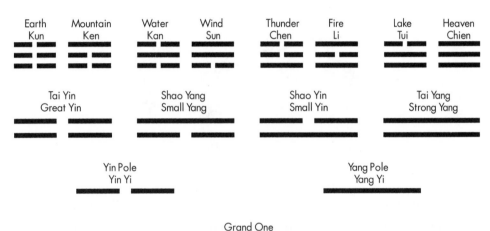

THE EIGHT TRIGRAMS ARE DIVIDED FROM THE GRAND ONE.

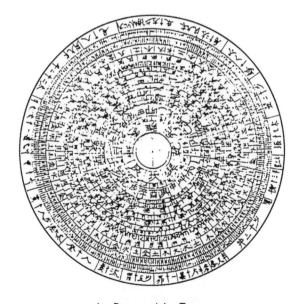

LO PAN, OR NET TABLET

The eight trigrams are used in different forms of Chinese and Japanese astrology and also in the Lo Shu, or magic square (see below). The eight directions and the center (the nine palaces) each have their typical quality. The central palace is above the earth axis and has the strongest effect on human energy and consciousness.

Taoist masters gave a name and a number to each of the nine stars and ascribed a unique quality to each of them.

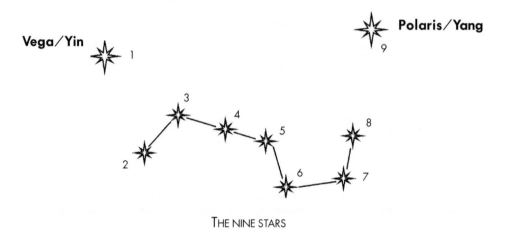

THE NINE STARS

According to our time of birth, each of us is more or less influenced by one of the nine stars, with its unique quality based on the five elements and the trigrams. During our lives we keep this basic quality but with time we will move to other positions in the magic square (called the houses), each with its unique influence on us. While being influenced, we are initiated into life's other possibilities.

4	9	2
3	5	7
8	1	6

THE MAGIC SQUARE ALWAYS ADDS UP TO FIFTEEN.

Your numbers are situated in the different palaces and will show you the universal quality that is influencing you the most at that specific moment.

The typical qualities of the nine palaces are:

Chen 3	Thunder: the arousing, the new impulse, exciting
Sun 4	Wind: the penetrating, gentleness
Li 9	Fire: clarity, conscious, independent
Kun 2	Earth: the receptive, trust, confidence, openness
Tui 7	Lake: joyfulness, fullness, satisfaction
Chien 6	Heaven: the creative, energetic, strong, light
Kan 1	Water: prudence, dangerous, unreliable
Ken 8	Mountain: keeping still, stability, rest
Chung 5	Female Trigram: Kun-black earth, the receptive
	Male Trigram: Ken-mountain, keeping still

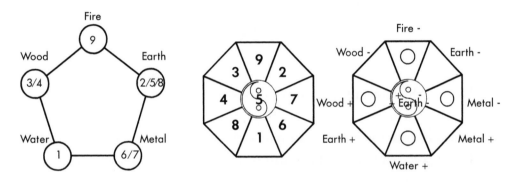

NUMEROLOGY IN THE *PA KUA* TRIGRAMS AND THE FIVE ELEMENTS

The five elements and eight trigrams of the *pa kua* are deeply interwoven into Chinese philosophy and astrology. The eight trigrams can be seen as a derivation of the five elements or as a derivation of the eight directions from the four.

The symbolism in the eight trigrams is interpreted in two different ways. One system is called the "preheavenly *pa kua*," defined by Fu Hsi during the age of the five legendary rulers (circa 2800 B.C.E.). The other is the "postheavenly *pa kua*," which originally came from King Wen of the Chou Dynasty (circa 1100 B.C.E.) in his book *Yixici*. This is the first written explanation of the relationship between the preheavenly *pa kua* and the postheavenly *pa kua*.

The preheavenly state is related to the time before the earth was formed, when everything was chaotic, like a cloud or mist. This is the state known as *Wu Chi*, a state in which nothing can be differentiated. The preheavenly state can also be seen as the period before the time that the earth started to materialize and heaven and earth began to separate (the Tai Chi or grand ultimate state). The postheavenly state begins at the time when heaven and earth were clearly distinguishable and the yin and yang poles were generated.

In human life the preheavenly and postheavenly states are separated by

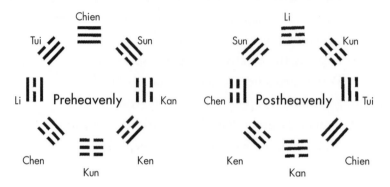

PREHEAVENLY *PA KUA* AND POSTHEAVENLY *PA KUA*

birth or the moment the baby can see the light or the sky. The goal of the Universal Tao practice is to unify the pre- and post-heavenly states of being. The quality of the preheavenly state is the basic energy of the newborn baby: totally soft, natural, and filled with its mother's essence, Chi, and blood. In addition, intuition, flexibility, softness, tenderness, and creativity are components of this preheavenly or childlike state. In some Taoist practices, five children are pictured as storing and crystallizing the pure virtue energy of the five elements.

Through the Universal Tao practices, the vital essences remain in the body until old age. The practitioner remains flexible, strong, and full of virtue. The unification of pre- and post-heavenly qualities is reached by first "training the postheaven to remedy the preheaven" and then "training the postheaven to return to the preheaven." In other words, we learn to harness, transform, and utilize our energy as living creatures in order to fully utilize our ability to return to the state of pure energy in which we lived before we manifested as human beings. In the unified state the body and mind become one, in accordance with the heavenly principles. Through meditation and exercises, the preheavenly mind will start to guide the postheavenly body so that the body will gradually return to its preheavenly state.

UNIFYING POSTHEAVEN INTO PREHEAVEN

The Ten Stems and Twelve Branches

As described before, the ten heavenly stems are the yin and yang poles of each of the five elements, while the twelve earthly branches are related to the twelve sections of the earth's rotation field projected onto the star world.

The sixty-year, stems-and-branches cycle occurs in correlation with the Jupiter/Saturn conjunction. The whole system describes geometrical coordinates in time and space, with Polaris as the center point and other celestial bodies used as additional references. The ten heavenly stems are often related with the planets and the five palaces in the star world.

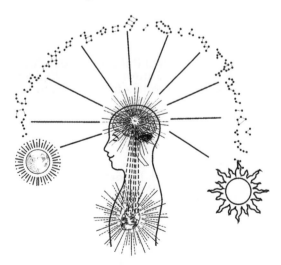

TEN STEMS IN THE SKY

Ten Stems						
No.	Name	Transcription	Significance Related			
1	甲	Chia	Yang moving in the East; sprouting	Fir Tree	}	Wood
2	乙	Yi	Plant growing in a crooked way; tendril; twig	Bamboo		
3	丙	Ping	Growth in southern heart; bloom	Torch-Flame	}	Fire
4	丁	Ting	Vegetation in warm season; summer	Lamp-Light		
5	戊	Wu	Exuberance; substance of life	Mountains	}	Earth
6	己	Ki	Winter; sleep, hibernation	Level Ground		
7	庚	Keng	Fullness of crops; the West; autumn harvest	Weapon	}	Metal
8	辛	Sin	Ripened fruit and its flavor; supposed to metallic	Cauldron		
9	壬	Jen	Yin at the height of its function; pregnancy	Willow	}	Water
10	癸	Kwei	Water absorbed by earth; Yang preparing for spring	Unruffled Stream		

ELEMENTS AND STEMS

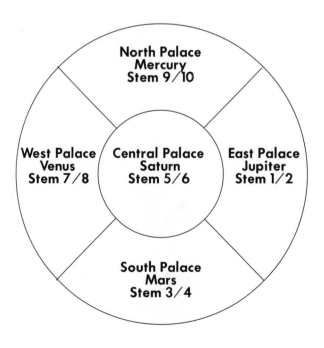

PALACES, PLANETS, AND STEMS

Taoist Astrology and the Structure of the Universe

36

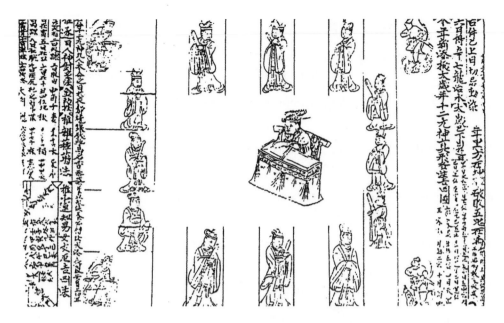

THE DEITIES OF THE TWELVE BRANCHES, FROM A TUN HUANG MANUSCRIPT DATED 978 C.E.

THE STRUCTURE OF THE UNIVERSE
AND THE PROCESS OF SPIRITUALIZATION

Evolving through the process of spiritualization, our spirit will enter different layers of universal consciousness. As discussed previously, the universe can be seen as consisting of three different realms: one of the pure law, one of Chi, and one of the manifestations of law and Chi.

We have all arrived on this planet through a materialization process: a contracting spiral that led us through these three realms into the physical, condensed form we have now. The materialization and condensation process continues after the moment of birth and through the various stages of physical development. The spiritual process, an expanding spiral that projects our spirit into the universe, progresses simultaneously.

When the level of consciousness grows, the intelligence and information network that connects each of us with the source will start to become more readily available and much easier for many people to feel. Thus we will, step by step, experience all the different dimensions of the universe, from our sexual energy to our spiritual origin.

It is easier to take seven steps one by one than to try to jump to the seventh step at once. The same is true for the spiritual process. We will

		Twelve Branches					Twelve Animals	
No.	Name	Transcription	Usual Meaning	Significance in the Duodenary cycle	Symbol	Related Element	Name	Meaning
1	子	Tze	Child	Regeneration of vegetation	Yang stirring underground	Water	鼠	Rat
2	丑	Chu	Cord	Relaxation; untying a knot	Hand half-opened		牛	Ox
3	寅	Yin	To revere	Awakening of life; plants	Wriggling earthworm		虎	Tiger
4	卯	Mao	A period of time	Breaking through the soil	Opening a gate	Wood	兔	Hare
5	辰	Chen	Vibration	First vegetation; seed-time	Thunderstorm		龍	Dragon
6	巳	Ssu	End	Supremacy of yang	Snake		蛇	Serpent
7	午	Wu	To oppose	Yin reasserting itself	Female principle in hidden growth	Fire	馬	Horse
8	未	Wei	Not yet	Taste of fruit	Tree in full bloom		羊	Goat
9	申	Shen	To expand	Yin growing strong	Clasped hands		猴	Monkey
10	酉	Yu	Ripe	Completion	Cider or wine-press	Metal	雞	Cock
11	戌	Shu	Guard	Exhaustion	Yang withdrawing underground		犬	Dog
12	亥	Hai	Kernel	Kernel or root	Yang in touch with yin	Water	猪	Boar

TWELVE BRANCHES AND TWELVE ANIMALS

gradually grow through the three realms step by step. The seven meditations in this book will guide you all the way through the manifested world of the earth, planets, and stars to the world of pure universal laws.

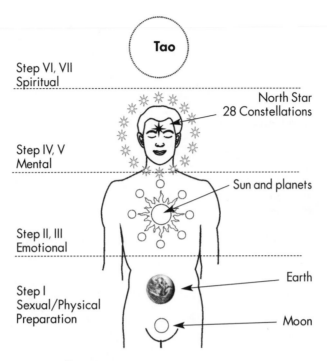

Step VI, VII
Spiritual

North Star
28 Constellations

Step IV, V
Mental

Sun and planets

Step II, III
Emotional

Step I
Sexual/Physical
Preparation

Earth

Moon

SEVEN STEPS OF THE SPIRITUAL PROCESS

Earth/Sun/Moon Triangle

Before we go on this journey, it is wise to take care of our vehicles. We will need to have healthy and strong bodies and to put on our safety belts. This is the rooting or connection to the earth. We also need to learn to control, transform, and use our sexual energy.

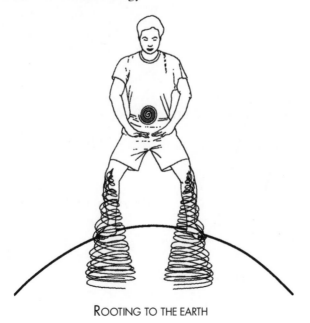

ROOTING TO THE EARTH

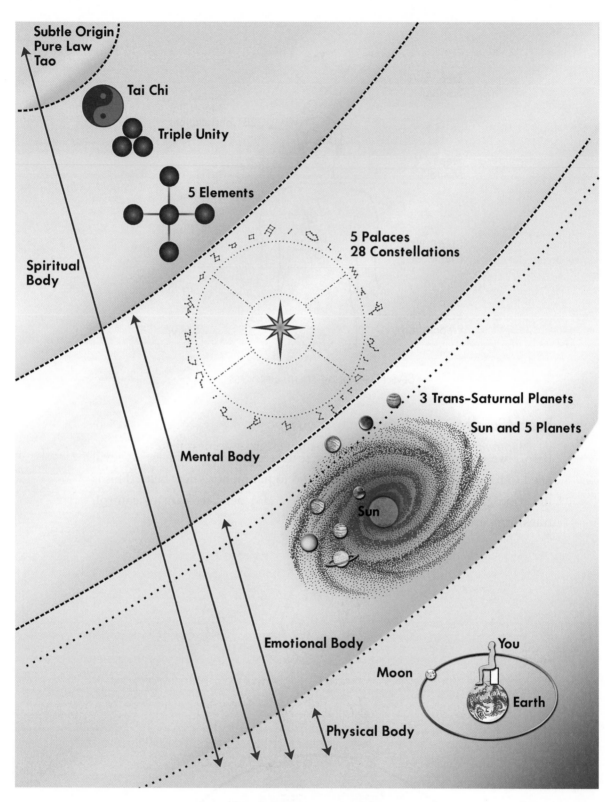

Subtle Origin
Pure Law
Tao

Tai Chi

Triple Unity

5 Elements

Spiritual
Body

5 Palaces
28 Constellations

3 Trans-Saturnal Planets

Sun and 5 Planets

Mental Body

Sun

Emotional Body

You

Moon

Earth

Physical Body

HUMAN ENERGY IN THE UNIVERSE

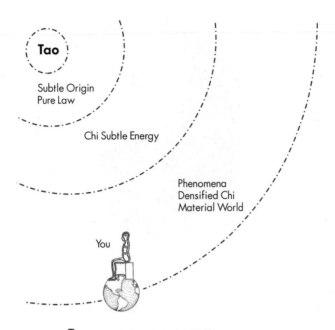

THREE REALMS IN THE UNIVERSE

Once we have built up a strong center in the lower Tan Tien, are enjoying a good connection with the earth, and have achieved control over our sexual energy through the basic practices and preparation exercises outlined in *Taoist Cosmic Healing*, we can begin expanding our awareness field.

The Universal Tao practices lead us step by step through the earth, universal, and cosmic realms. Without these preparations, the effects of our planetary and stellar meditations will be limited, as we lack the power to attract, absorb, and integrate the energy in our physical body.

If you have not done any Universal Tao practices, you *can* do the planetary/stellar meditations—however, you will have to build up your physical body, lower Tan Tien, and the star/planet connection simultaneously. Keep this balance. Build up the time spent doing practice slowly and regularly.

The centering, rooting, and cultivation process of the physical body and the sexual energy should be continuously developed because these abilities and energies are further utilized as we expand and grow with the universe. In this way, we become like a big tree with deep roots and develop the ability to draw information and energy from the universe down into the earthly realm and physical body. The figure on the opposite page, "Human Energy in the Universe," illustrates how we can visualize our relationship to the universal picture.

Sexual energy is connected to the moon. The sun and the moon energies are easily experienced because we can see and feel them with our earthly senses. Yet most people do not consciously experience the effects of the

Sun, Love,
Consciousness

Moon, Sexual Energy,
Unconsciousness

SUN AND MOON BALANCE

moon. We cannot touch it like the earth or feel its radiant energy as easily as the heat from the sun.

The goal of our meditative practices is to tune in to the energy frequencies and awareness field of the planets and stars and integrate these into our physical body. The moon is an important step in the development of our universal awareness because the moon meditation triggers deeply hidden layers of the unconscious mind connected with our sexual potential.

Our connection with the moon will help us to become profoundly aware of our sexual essence, to which we cannot relate with our ordinary mind. Through the moon and sun meditations, the sexual essence that is stored deep inside the sexual organs and kidneys becomes available and transforms from unconsciousness into consciousness, and from Jing (essence) into Shen (spirit).

When we suppress or have no control over our sexual energy, the earth energy will be insufficient for us to keep balance and be stable enough to advance in the spiritual process. Unconsciously or consciously, a part of us may be blocked by sexual frustration and its associated emotions. All people in the modern world have a layer of heaviness and negativity on the level of their sexuality. This is based on the social/collective conditioning of many centuries of religious and scientific control.

The cool moon energy in the lower body is balanced by the contact with the warm sun energy in the upper body. The sun will help us to open the heart center and feel connected to nature, the universe, and other people. The sun is the central point of the solar system and governs a higher awareness than the other planets. The sun is a star in the planet world and a gate out of the planetary emotional and rational mind layer into the realm of the higher mind and the spirit. The sun and the moon energies need to be balanced to create peace between the love and sex energies and between the conscious and unconscious. The figure opposite illustrates this balance of the sun and moon energies.

Further Steps in Our Universal Awareness Journey

The first step in our universal awareness journey involves building a strong center in the lower Tan Tien, developing a firm connection with the earth, and achieving control over our sexual energy. This prepares us for balancing the energies of the sun and moon.

Step two on this journey leads us deeper into our solar system, to the sun and the five basic planets. The five basic planets (Mars, Saturn, Venus, Mercury, Jupiter) are a materialized form of the energy of the five elements. In the planetary world we find the sources of our collective emotional and lower mental tendencies. First we connect with the sun and the five basic planets, then we connect with and integrate their specific frequencies and their qualities/virtues.

In step three we expand further out to the border of our solar system into the three planets beyond Saturn (Uranus, Neptune, and Pluto). These three planets represent the emotional, social consciousness that has recently formed (over the last few centuries) as well as the development of society and social awareness.

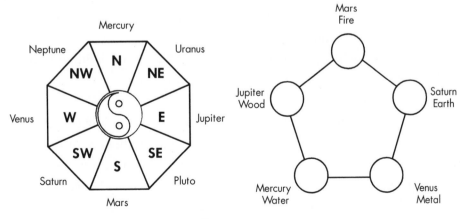

FIVE ELEMENTS

According to the Taoist tradition, the five closest planets can also represent the five elements. If we add the three planets beyond Saturn, we can link the eight planets with the eight trigrams of the *pa kua* and the eight directions. Since Chinese astrologers did not originally know about Uranus, Neptune, and Pluto, the use of the eight planets must have been introduced in this century. Chinese astrology also uses some additional planets known as "counter planets," which are nonmaterialized energetic formations.

The fourth step in our journey leads us to the world of the stars, star clouds, and milky ways. This represents a finer quality of energy that is related to the higher world of the mind and the spirit. As we noted previously, Taoist masters observed that the North Star always keeps its position while the twenty-eight constellations turn around it. For this reason Taoists have always seen the North Star as the center of the star world and also as the gate to the spiritual realm and the Tao. In the planetary and stellar meditation, we first connect with the North Star. In this way we deeply penetrate into the star world. Then connections with galaxies are established, which are related to the five palaces and five elements.

Astronomical observation of the twelve or twenty-eight constellations, combined with intensive meditation on the individual qualities of these signs, can deepen our connection with the star world and can greatly accelerate our spiritual advancement. This is, however, a quite advanced and complex practice.

In step five, we will combine the two most extreme poles in the star world: the ultra yang force of a quasar and the ultra yin force of a black hole. We will use an uplifting spiral of these two to project an awareness in the pure yang unmanifested world in order to multiply our intention.

When we reach the sixth step, we go beyond the realm of phenomena and the realm of Chi into the realm of the spiritual laws, the five elements, the triple unity, polarity, and the pure law.

Step seven is what we call "being and living the source continuously in a state of absolute freedom." We could also call this level "zero" because all separation will end in this state.

The figure on page 40 illustrates the structure of the universe and how the different layers in the universe are connected to our bodies. In step seven, the energy cores of these different layers are all lined up on the "central thrusting channel" that is located in the center of the body between the perineum and the crown. The connection and integration of the essence of these core points into our body will automatically raise our energy and awareness level and trigger the connection with more subtle universal frequencies. In this way our body and the universe become one. Our presence and all our actions become an effortless reflection of the Tao itself.

Each of the seven steps described in this section is accompanied by major changes in all aspects of the practitioner's life.

Astronomical Overview

HOW TO USE THE ASTRONOMICAL INFORMATION IN THIS BOOK

Astronomy is a valuable tool for understanding and cultivating our relationship with the material universe. The accumulation of astronomical knowledge does not, of course, guarantee a higher energy and awareness level. The information presented may help you create a direct, experiential link between where you are living now on the earth and the heavenly energies of planets and stars. Only when this direct, experiential contact is made can the study of and meditation on the universe improve your quality of life.

In this chapter, we will summarize some basic astronomical facts. They are meant to increase your understanding of the world of stars and planets. If we study some basic astronomy and use it to expand our awareness, our intellectual mind will be more satisfied and will be able to function as a vehicle that can travel beyond time and space. Together with the accompanying pictures, this information is presented to give you some specific connection points during the meditations. After you have studied the information, simply put the picture in front of you and take it in deeply. Empty the mind of all other activity. Then close your eyes, expand your awareness, and, with your intention, travel in space. Be aware that the physical objects you are connecting to are just the materialized centers of an energy field or belt. It is the frequency and the energy in the belt that you are tuning into. So, relax.

Keep your hands on the lower Tan Tien and keep the energy deep inside. Repeat this process four to five times until you start to feel the connection. Use the meditation techniques that are described in chapter 10.

THE FORMATION OF THE SOLAR SYSTEM

Planet Earth is a small planet that has a 365-day cycle around a middle-sized star, the sun. There are nine planets in our solar system. Together with the planetoids, satellites, comets, meteors, and some gas and dust formations, they form our solar system.

The sun is ten times as big as the biggest planet in our solar system (Jupiter) and more than a hundred times larger than the earth. Since the mass of the sun is 330,000 times greater than that of the earth, its gravitational force holds the earth in a fixed yearly cycle. Many believe the birth of the solar system was introduced by the implosion of a cloud of gas and dust. The reason for this implosion is still a mystery, but meteor analysis shows that an exploding star or supernova might have caused it.

Our solar system started its materialization process about four and a half to five billion years ago. Around that time, a cloud charged with cosmic dust gathered at the edge of the Milky Way. The centripetal force in the cloud caused the formation of a more dense center. This created heat, which speeded up the rotational force and flattened the form. After millions of years, the immense gathering of energy in the center caused a nuclear reaction and self-combustion. At other places in this cloud, smaller concentrations of gas and cosmic dust gathered as a result of the lower density. They did not inflame but materialized.

The specific location and orbit of each planet in our solar system is determined by a balance point between the rotation force/centrifugal force and the gravitational force /centripetal force in relation to the sun. The planets closer to the sun were baked and became very hard because the gases were dispersed by the heat and the ion/electron wind sent into the universe by the sun. Further out from the sun, the temperature is much lower. The planets there materialized into big balls of fluid gas with a vast center, often with a crust of frozen substance.

Expansion and Contraction of the Solar System

Astronomical studies tell us that there are billions of galaxies in the universe and that there are also billions of stars in most of these galaxies. Our solar system travels through the universe at a speed of about 300 kilometers per second. Even at this speed it takes about 230 million years for our solar system to make a complete cycle through the Milky Way. During this cycle, or *galactic year*, the solar system is not always at the same distance from the center of the Milky Way.

When the solar system is closer to the center, this is called the *galactic summer*. Our solar system responds to the stronger contractile force at this

Gas cloud

Gas concentration around core

Spontaneous self-combustion

Formation of other planets

Solar system now

FORMATION OF THE SOLAR SYSTEM

Astronomical Overview

47

point in the galactic year. The planets come closer to the sun in this period, and the atmosphere heats up, which enhances the size of the flora and fauna. When the solar system is further away from the center of the Milky Way, the solar system expands, so a greater distance arises between the earth and the sun. This creates lower temperatures, and plants and animal species will be smaller. It is generally believed that the first life forms on earth appeared some 3.2 billion years ago. Since that time, the earth has completed about thirteen cycles through the Milky Way.

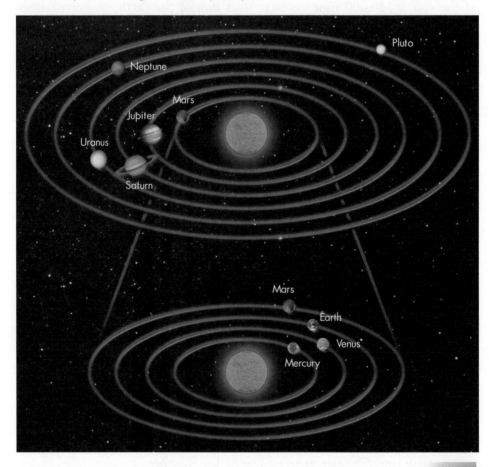

OVERVIEW OF THE SOLAR SYSTEM

OVERVIEW OF THE PLANETS IN OUR SOLAR SYSTEM

EARTH

Planet Earth is a blue planet with a moderately humid climate and a slightly unstable surface, 70 percent of which is covered by water. Its atmosphere consists mainly of nitrogen and oxygen. Under the approximately 32-kilometer-thick crust we find a 3,000-kilometer-thick inner mantle. The core of the earth is a moving sea of liquid nickel and iron, which creates a strong electromagnetic field. It rotates around its axis in one day and the sun's in one year.

MOON

The moon is a satellite of the earth. Since the moon has no protective atmosphere, it has been bombarded by objects in space for the last 800 million years. The craters that we can see from the earth are the "scars" of this activity, their presence sustained by the absence of erosion. Stones have been found on the moon that are more than four billion years old, the same age as the solar system. The origin of the moon in relation to the earth is still a mystery. Its rotational speeds around its axis and around the earth are about equal—twenty-eight days. For this reason we always see the same side of the moon. Temperatures on the moon vary from between +127°C and -173°C.

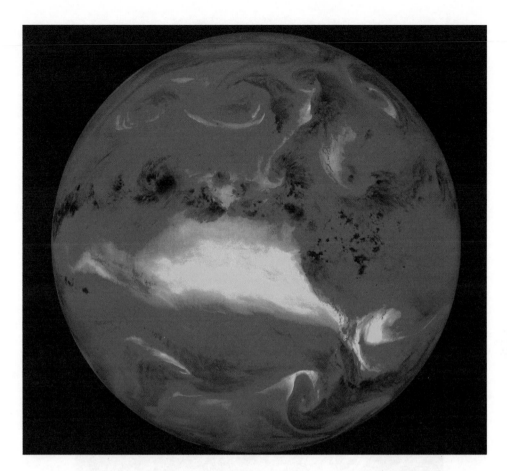

SUN

The sun is the giant of our solar system, with a bigger mass than all of the planets put together. Compared to other stars it is small- to medium-sized. It is the main light source in our solar system and in this way generates life on our planet. Its main components are hydrogen and helium. The sun radiates enormous amounts of light particles and radioactivity. It turns around its axis in 246 days. The temperature in the center of the sun is approximately 15 million °C. Each second the sun radiates more energy than man has used since the beginning of civilization.

MERCURY

Mercury is like a giant cinder with a deeply pockmarked surface. Its proximity to the sun has caused its atmosphere to be burned away completely. On the sunny side the temperature rises to 430°C; on the dark side it drops to -170°C. It orbits the sun in 88 days and rotates around its axis in 58.6 days. The marked surface may also be the effect of shrinkage.

VENUS

In the past, Venus was called both the "clear morning star" and the "clear evening star." The reason for this is that Venus swings across our "planetary view" over a period of about sixteen months. For about eight months it is visible in the morning, and the other eight months it is visible in the evening. Its surface is covered by a thick atmosphere, and surface temperatures rise to 500°C. The atmosphere allows sunlight in but not out, which causes a greenhouse effect. A constant acid rain (carbon dioxide and sulfuric acid) falls from the clouds. It orbits the sun in 225 days and rotates around its axis in 243 days. The pressure of its atmosphere is about 90 times greater than that of Earth's.

MARS

The red planet Mars is a giant sand desert where huge storms occur regularly. It also has ice caps on the poles, just like Earth, and has several giant volcanoes. The highest volcano is two and a half times as high as Mount Everest. Mars has a thin, pink atmosphere and a deep, red surface. Temperatures are between +20°C and -140°C. It orbits the sun in 687 days. A Martian day also takes about twenty-four hours. It may have had water on its surface and a denser atmosphere in the past.

JUPITER

Jupiter is the largest planet in the solar system, with a diameter nine times greater than the earth's. Because it is visible throughout the night, the Greeks called the planet the supreme god. Giant storms with wind speeds of 350 kilometers per hour lash the dust from the surface and send it up to 25 kilometers in the air. The atmosphere contains mainly hydrogen. Just like the sun, its composition is nine parts hydrogen to one part helium, but because of its smaller mass, it never self-ignited. Its surface temperature is between +25°C and -150°C; the center is about 20,000°C. If its mass were fifty times greater, we would have had two stars in our solar system, creating a completely different environment. Jupiter has sixteen satellites.

SATURN

Saturn is a pale yellow giant that looks a little like Jupiter. It has a similar atmosphere and also has huge storms. Wind speeds of more than 1,500 kilometers per hour have been measured. It is surrounded by thousands of rings (containing ice and rocks), making it look like an old gramophone record. The temperatures on its surface are around -150°C. It is the lightest planet in our solar system. If we could drop it in water it would float. Seventeen satellites have been discovered around Saturn.

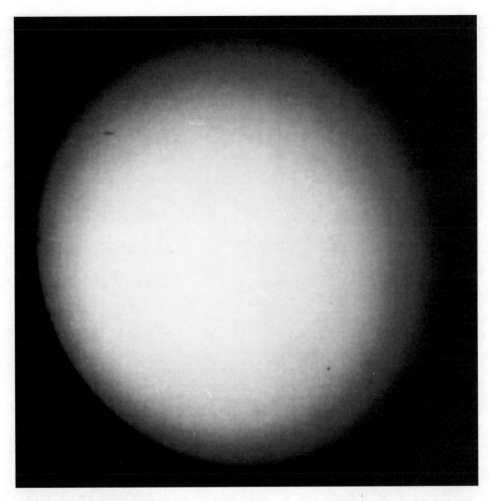

URANUS

Uranus is the only planet that lies on its side as it revolves around the sun. It is invisible to the naked eye and was unknown until 1781. The astronomer William Herschel discovered it with the use of a telescope. According to scientific models, the outer layer consists of hydrogen and helium, which covers a layer of partially solid methane, ammonia, and water. The interior is said to consist of a stony center of metals and silicate. The surface temperature is around -215°C. It has a diffuse belt of rings and fifteen satellites.

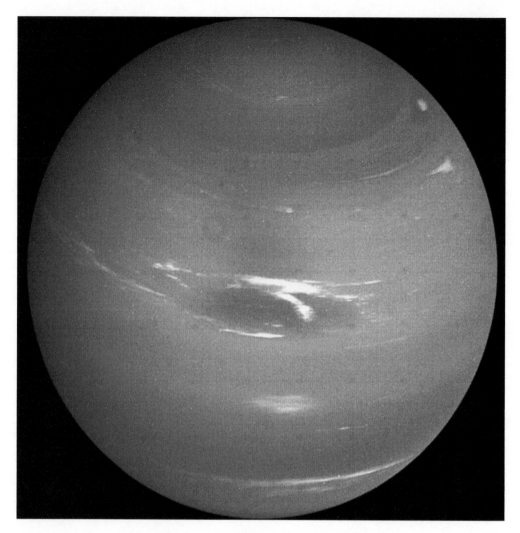

NEPTUNE

Neptune's existence was predicted by mathematicians who calculated that the deviations observed in the orbit of Uranus could only be explained by the gravitational pull of an unknown, more distant planet. In 1846, Johann Gotfried Galle discovered Neptune where the mathematicians calculated it should be. Neptune is said to have a very similar structure and composition to the earth.

PLUTO

Clyde Tombaugh discovered Pluto in 1930. It orbits the sun at a distance of about 6 billion kilometers. It has a diameter of about 2,300 kilometers (the earth's moon is 3,476 kilometers in diameter) and a mass 0.002 times that of the Earth. This frozen stone clump has a thin atmosphere of methane and a surface temperatures of -210°C. It has an orbital angle of 17°, which is unique in the planetary world. It also has a strong elliptical orbit, causing a crossing of the Neptune orbit.

The inner part of the solar system contains four similar, rocky planets: Mercury, Venus, Earth, and Mars. This is followed by an asteroid belt containing millions of irregularly shaped stones. Further out are the four gas/ice giants: Jupiter, Saturn, Uranus, and Neptune. Pluto is the planet farthest out in our solar system. It is a comparatively small, frozen rock that might previously have been a satellite of Neptune. Many astrologists and astronomers talk about a tenth planet being even farther out in the solar system. This planet would have a mass two to five times greater than the earth's. This would explain the deviations in the orbits of the outer planets. Since Pluto's mass is very small, another planet is probably causing this effect. The angle of the tenth planet's orbit would probably be about 75°.

The *planetary field* is the central area in our solar system. It is a small part of the total area of our solar system. The outer edge of our solar system almost touches other solar systems. The nearest solar system is Alpha Centauri. The many solar systems in our galaxy rotate around the center of the Milky Way at a speed of 300 kilometers per second. It takes more than 200 million years to finish a complete cycle around the center of our Milky Way.

It is not accidental that the three outer planets (Uranus, Neptune, and Pluto) were only discovered during the last 150 years. As human evolution moves toward the "center of the spiral" and as we return to our divine origin, we experience an increasing speed of events (reaching a peak around 2100). We find that as the solar systems in our galaxy spiral around the Milky Way, we as humans seem to be spiraling back to our original knowledge as well. This whirlpool of events strongly activates the collective-consciousness field. If the body's energy system and the soul connection are not developed, the activated collective-consciousness field and the three trans-Saturnal planets can create a great deal of confusion, exhaustion, and mental and emotional imbalance. But, if we can integrate the cosmic forces with who we are as humans, they will trigger unique human abilities at the level of mind and spirit and the collective, social consciousness.

In 1977 a large, asteroid-like planet was discovered. It has an irregular orbit, at times coming nearer the sun than Uranus and at others extending far beyond Pluto. In this way, this planet connects the personal planets with the trans-Saturnal planets, which are related to the collective consciousness. Astronomers named it Chiron, which is the name of a Greek mythological figure that was half human and half horse. It is a symbol for healing. Also, since 1977, healing arts have rapidly developed and spread on our planet.

As time goes by, more universal knowledge will be gained. This is always connected to related changes in personal and collective consciousness.

STARS AND GALAXIES

Images taken recently through the Hubble space telescope show the different stages in the birth process of stars. These pictures show that the powerful energy, ultraviolet radiation, and high-speed gas clouds unleashed by adult stars trigger the birth of new stars in the surroundings. Ultraviolet light emitted by the neighbor stars energizes the gas clouds. Inside these huge, interstellar gas columns, the density can become so high that gravity takes over and causes the gas clouds to collapse and split into smaller clumps or gas eggs. When compression continues, the pressure and temperature in the clouds may rise to the point where nuclear fusion ignites their cores so that they become fledgling stars.

After this point is reached, a star will shine for millions of years. A star like the sun can live for over 10 billion years. Bigger stars are often burned out after 20 billion years. Generally speaking, we can say that the younger stars are violet/blue in color, the middle-aged ones are yellowish, the older ones are red-brown, and the oldest are black. According to the estimated age of many stars, it is clear that our Milky Way must be over 12 billion years old.

As a star ages, it might turn into a white dwarf due to lack of fuel. It also can explode and become a supernova, a star that is as bright as 10 billion suns. The third possibility is implosion into a black hole, a concentration of density and gravity so extreme that no matter, radiation, or light can escape from it.

Other kinds of stars include pulsars and quasars. Astronomers believe that pulsars are fast-rotating neutron stars that radiate light (or sound waves or radioactive waves) in a beam that we detect every time it is directed toward the earth. Quasars are the brightest sky objects in the visible universe. They often shine with a brightness of 200 billion suns and often are visible with the unaided eye even though they are at a distance of billions of light years.

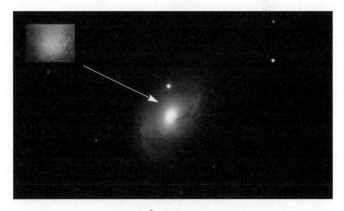

SUPERNOVA

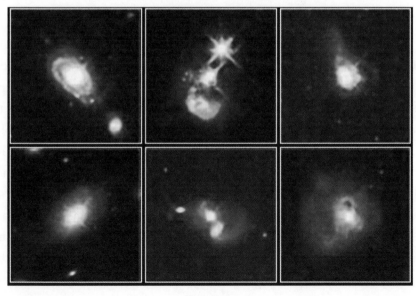

QUASARS

Astronomical Overview

Earth is located about one-third of the way from the outside border of our galaxy. The galaxy has a diameter of about 100,000 light years and contains about 100 billion stars. The biggest concentration of stars is found in the central area. There are billions of other galaxies in the universe. When we look into the night sky, some of the stars we are seeing are in fact galaxies composed of billions of stars. These galaxies are grouped into clusters and in turn these clusters belong to super clusters. Our galaxy belongs to a group of about thirty other galaxies called "the local group." The closest other big galaxy is the Andromeda nebula, which is about 2,200,000 light years away. This means that the light we now see and measure from this galaxy was emitted 2.2 million years ago. On a dark, clear night, we can see the Andromeda nebula without binoculars or a telescope.

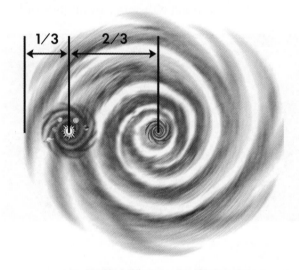

OUR SOLAR SYSTEM IN THE MILKY WAY

In Taoist astrology the sky is divided by twenty-eight or sixty-four constellations. Modern astrologers often use the different distances of the stars in one constellation as proof that there is a connection between the stars in that constellation and that, in this way, the constellation affects the human condition. However, the real distance of the stars is just one aspect of the unique quality of each constellation. The angle of the constellation, as seen from the earth, also informs the sense of connection between the stars and their specific group energy. In the Big Dipper, the five most central stars belong to the star cluster that is closest to us, which is at a distance of between fifty-nine and seventy-five light years. The outer two stars are not in this cluster and are at a greater distance.

DIFFERENT GALACTIC FORMS

There are many different types of galaxies, but they are mostly divided into three main groups.

SPIRAL GALAXIES

Spiral galaxies, like the Milky Way, have a central elliptical region filled with many old stars. Around this center there is a sphere of old stars connected with the outer spiral arms, which are composed of younger stars and regions of gas and dust where stars are still being born.

ELLIPTICAL GALAXIES

Elliptical galaxies contain very few young stars or gas and dust. They are mainly composed of older groupings of stars. Few stars are born here.

IRREGULAR GALAXIES

Irregular galaxies are those without a particular form. One of these is the large Magellanic Cloud, the companion of our solar system.

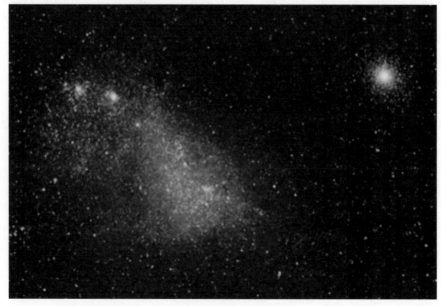

MAGELLANIC CLOUD

Taoist Star Practices and Their Effect on Human Awareness

THE NORTH STAR AND BIG DIPPER IN THE TAOIST MEDITATION PRACTICES

Ancient practices viewed the stars as great sources of the subtle energy of Chi as well as material manifestations of Chi. The manifestation of the stars in brilliance, pulsation, and color shows the constant interaction of universal/ heavenly energy and the more material energy. The sun is seen as the fullest form of pure, yang energy, which is present to a lesser degree in the other stars. In the stars, we find high concentrations of the vital, primal essence, or Chi. The kind of Chi that stars produce is abundant and readily available for use in the Cosmic Healing form of Chi Kung. Because of their inherent relation to the embryonic essence (like the sexual essence in our body), stars were seen as forms of water energy. The expression of bright, white light also shows the inherent metal energy. In *Taoist Cosmic Healing* we learned that the healing color of the lungs is white, and that its corresponding element is metal. When one familiarizes oneself with the elements and the healing colors, one can begin to see the energetic connection in all living things.

For the Taoists, stars are the places where immortal beings reside— mostly in the central star palace, but also in other locations. (The central palace is the region of the heavens above the North Pole. The stars of the Big Dipper, Polaris, and Vega all lie within the central palace.) The appearance of newborn stars demonstrates that a high master has made the transition to heaven. One Taoist master during the Han dynasty (206 B.C.E.–220 C.E.),

Ching Fong, predicted that after his death a new star would appear in the constellation Hercules, and indeed, a supernova suddenly appeared just after he died.

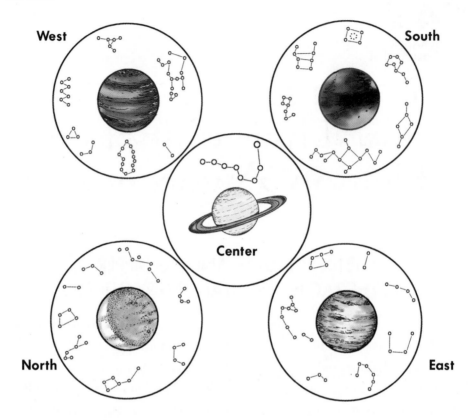

FIVE PLANETS, DIRECTIONS, AND CONSTELLATIONS

The Taoist masters viewed the North Star and Big Dipper as the greatest sources of stellar power. These stars were believed to be great sources of supernatural energy and "yang luminosity." The North Star has been used by many enlightened Taoist masters as the ultimate gate to the Tao. This North Star gate was used in meditation practices while preparing for death and finally at the moment of dying. Other spiritual systems also use connection points or gates into the sky.

The Chinese emperors were seen as heavenly children. Many stars around the North Star have the name of an emperor or one of his family members. The great emperors were often depicted with the Big Dipper in one hand and the North Star in the other.

Because the earth's axis wobbles every 26,000 years (approximately), different stars get aligned over the earth axis. This means that different stars take the position of the "north star" during different periods. In about 12,000 years, Vega will once again be our "north star." From 1000 to 500 B.C.E. it was the star Kochab; during the time the Egyptian pyramids were being built it was Dra Thuban; about 13,000 years ago it was Vega. During the Ming dynasty it was Tianshu.

A name that is generally used for pole stars is *zhong ji*, "the center of heaven." Another name is *tai yi*, "the great one." The function of the North Star is to emit the essence, the embryonic energy flow. The North Star has a close connection to the seven stars of the Big Dipper. The North Star is found along the line projected from the seventh and eighth Big Dipper stars. Traditionally the Big Dipper/North Star axis was used to mark the seasons. The North Star/Big Dipper axis moves through the "four palaces" during the four seasons. The Big Dipper is also a vehicle for the energy of the North Star. When the spiritual essence of the *tai yi*, or North Star, spills over, the Dipper holds and transmits its essence through its seven bright gates of celestial power.

In the Taoist advanced practices, the North Star and Big Dipper energies are connected with the different bones of the skull. Through this connection with the points of the skull, the connection with the universal Chi, or universal light, is deeply integrated in the brain and the glands within the skull (see the "crystal palace," page 68). Each of the seven stars of the Big Dipper has a connection with the lower planetary world (the five planets, sun, and moon)

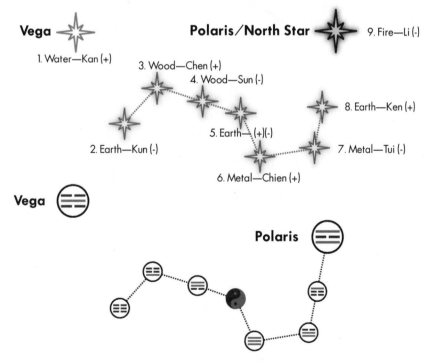

NORTH STAR, VEGA, BIG DIPPER, AND FIVE ELEMENTS

as well as with the higher vibrational world of the five elements and the *pa kua* trigrams. According to the oracle texts of the Han dynasty, each of the Big Dipper stars has a unique earthly manifestation in the animal and plant kingdoms. The seven-star principle is not unique to the Big Dipper. It can also be found in the Pleiades, the Vermilion Bird, and other constellations.

In one type of Taoist astrology, the numbers *1* to *9* and the nine energies of the *pa kua* (the eight directions and the center) were used as a form of numerology connected to the seven stars of the Big Dipper, Polaris, and Vega. Since the star Vega, which is related to number 1, was known as a star related to destruction, it was not used with the crystal palace.

In Taoism, it is believed that nine stars compose the "true Dipper." These include the seven familiar ones and two hidden or invisible ones. According to one source these hidden stars hold the embryonic essence (Jing) and actualizing spirit (Shen). A practice from the T'ang dynasty (618–907 C.E.) that is still used in China today is a practice of visualizing the nine stars of the Dipper and the star Alcor while holding the breath. Similar to the principle of counterplanets in Chinese astrology and the modern astronomical hypothesis that quasars and black holes function together, some Taoists believe that there are nine black stars counterbalancing the nine Big Dipper stars.

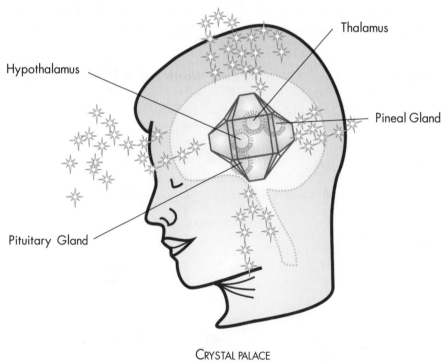

Thalamus

Hypothalamus

Pineal Gland

Pituitary Gland

CRYSTAL PALACE

In the Universal Tao meditation practices, we use the combined energy of the North Star and the Big Dipper to connect with the universal light, or universal Chi.

The Big Dipper light (red) is absorbed by the thalamus and hypothalamus glands while the North Star light (violet) relates to the pineal gland. The pineal gland is our internal compass, while the North Star is our external compass. Taoist masters believed that if the North Star was able to keep all the constellations in orbit, its size and mass must be enormous.

In Taoist astrology, twenty-eight constellations are ordered around the North Star and the Big Dipper. In each of the twenty-eight days of the moon cycle, one of the constellations reaches its maximum influence. The special magnetic field of the moon and earth energies, combined together, attracts the fine star energies and creates a special spiritual condition on our planet.

Besides the twenty-eight constellations around the North Star, there are billions of galaxies, each with billions of stars. All these stars have a direct connection with the billions of cells in our body, where at the moment of fertilization and birth a specific position gives you a unique energetic charge and direction in life.

Through meditation practices and through integrating new insights and higher awareness into your daily life, the information from the stars and your personal cells becomes synchronized. This brings you back to your true task in this life, but it also gives you access to the universal information field. The direct connection with this intelligence will naturally provide you with all the information and life force required for you to fulfill your true life task.

EARTH AXIS WOBBLING AND POLESHIFTS

The earth has three movements: it rotates around the sun (one year); it rotates around its own axis (one day); and the axis wobbles, called *precession* (one full cycle takes approximately 26,000 years). The projection of the earth's two axes to the north creates a circular form between Vega and Polaris. There is a strong electromagnetic belt around the earth due to its rotational force. This belt is strongest around the equator and weakest at the poles. The South Pole is directed toward the center of the Milky Way while the North Pole is directed toward the outside of the Milky Way. For this reason the energy that comes through the North Pole is clearer and more subtle than that which comes from the South Pole. The northern sky is governed by the energy of the North Star and its twenty-eight constellations, and is considered richer in terms of star and galactic energies.

The earth's rotation around its axis creates a strong electromagnetic field. The wobbling of the earth's axis creates different stellar influences with enormous effects on the conditions of our planet.

EARTH'S ROTATION

The wobbling movement of the axis of the earth has a strong effect on human civilization and the quality of life on earth. It takes approximately 26,000 years for the earth to make a full 360° precession cycle. The strongest activation of energy occurs when the axis is directed straight toward Polaris. Around the year 2102, the North Star will be in perfect line with the earth axis. This will highly increase the influence of spiritual energy on our planet.

The *galactic year* is the movement of our solar system around the center of the Milky Way. Our solar system moves through the galaxy at a speed of 300 kilometers per second, taking 230 million years to make a complete cycle around the center of the galaxy. During different phases of this cycle, our solar system will be located at different distances from the center, which will create varying gravitational conditions in the solar system and on our planet, and which defines the different galactic "seasons."

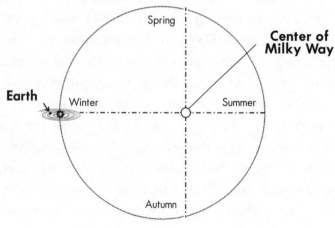

GALACTIC YEAR (230 MILLION YEARS)

The energy of Polaris is the yang energy from heaven related to the *governing vessel*. The energy of Vega is the yin energy from heaven related to the *conception vessel*. The governing vessel is the line of energy that runs up the spine, and the conception vessel is the line of energy that runs down the front of the torso. When we connect these two lines of energy, we have what is called the *Microcosmic Orbit*.

During the 26,000-year precession cycle, the period in which the earth's axis is pointed toward Polaris is traditionally seen as the "light" period. This is a time of flourishing spiritual life on earth and a period of happiness and good luck. The period in which the earth's axis is pointed toward Vega (13,000 years later) is seen as the "dark" period, with destruction of society and a low spiritual level on our planet.

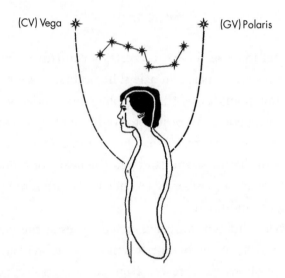

NINE STARS AND GOVERNING AND CONCEPTION VESSELS

When Polaris is above the earth axis, the crystal palace (pituitary gland) within the skull receives information from the governing vessel and transfers it to the conception vessel, whereby it is integrated. Thus energy is brought up the back line of the Microcosmic Orbit (the governing vessel), is affected by Polaris, via the crystal palace, and then sent back down the front channel (the conception vessel). Every time we circulate Chi in the Microcosmic Orbit while consciously connecting with Polaris, we enhance this Chi. When Vega is above our earth axis, the energy is directly absorbed into the lower centers without the spiritual/universal connection. The result is isolation, arrogance, and destruction.

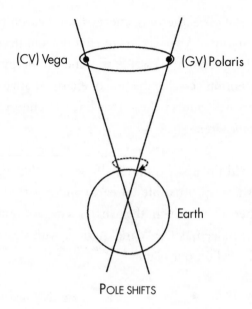

(CV) Vega   (GV) Polaris

Earth

POLE SHIFTS

The rotational force of the earth creates a centrifugal force. When this expanding force reaches a peak, an axis shift occurs. If we roll an egg away from us, at a certain point it may start wobbling and suddenly rotate, creating another axis and new poles. According to some sources, several of these sudden pole shifts have occurred on earth. These shifts happen in a few days, creating giant shifts of the water and land and the death of millions of humans and animals. There are a number of legends from different civilizations that describe these shifts and floods.

There are many different influences affecting us at the same time. All of these influences have a unique rhythm. It is the correlation of all these rhythms, influences, and positions that creates a unique universal condition at every moment of our lives. Taoist astrologers believe that another strong influence on human awareness is the *photon belt*, which is believed to be a large band of intense photon (light) energy that is moving through the universe. Photons are very small particles of electromagnetic energy, without mass or electrical charge, and of an indefinable life span. These photons are in our atmosphere all the time, but their number is gradually increasing because our planet is believed to be traveling through the photon belt for greater periods of time every year. From the year 2013, we will be constantly surrounded by and immersed in these photons for a period of about two thousand years. The increasing influence of the North Star and of the photon belt represents a unique spiritual possibility for all of us. The North American Indians, Mayans, Tibetans, and Egyptians were among the ancient cultures that were quite aware of the age of light that would begin at the start of the twenty-first century.

UNIVERSAL TAO PRACTICES THAT CONNECT US WITH UNIQUE UNIVERSAL CONDITIONS

The strong Polaris energy, which carries the information of all the stars of the northern sky, shines straight down into the crown. It has a direct connection with the thrusting channels, the important energy channels that run through the central part of the body between the crown and the perineum.

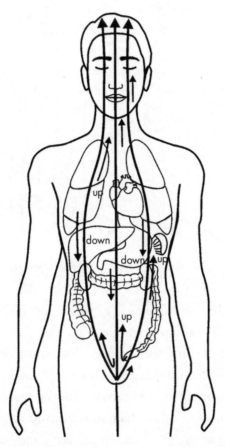

THREE THRUSTING CHANNELS: CHI ENERGY CAN FLOW UP OR DOWN.

There are three thrusting channels: one central, one left, and one right. They create a left/right balance and a direct vertical connection between all the important organs. The influence of the spiritual activation of the Polaris energy is already quite apparent in present human behavior and interest. More and more people are attracted to meditation, spirituality, and self-development. In the next century, their number and the depth of their spiritual growth will certainly increase.

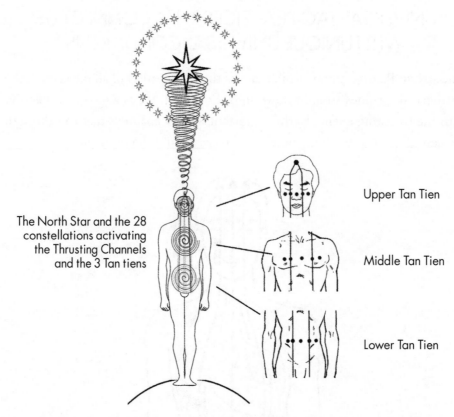

The North Star and the 28 constellations activating the Thrusting Channels and the 3 Tan tiens

Upper Tan Tien

Middle Tan Tien

Lower Tan Tien

POLARIS ENERGY CONNECTING WITH THREE TAN TIENS AND THRUSTING CHANNELS

Another clear sign that humanity is quickly moving toward a new phase in its evolution and into a new direction is the fact that many things in society are changing at a dazzling speed. More than at any time before in human history, the pace of life has quickened. Many people feel highly pressured and confused as they desperately try to keep up with the changes in all dimensions of social life, with encompassing changes occurring in such domains as science and technology, family ties, communications, and security. Many people experience this whirlpool of change as a direct challenge to their currently weak condition and as a major reason for loss of energy.

The arrival of the forthcoming period of light, in connection with the North Star activation, should be seen as a powerful opportunity for us to actively engage in further development and growth. Although the transformation of energy is in principle available to everybody, our overall condition and focus will greatly determine the level to which we will be able to integrate the newly arising energy conditions in the universe. Our health and freedom greatly depend on our ability to follow and integrate these universal changes. In the same way as an amoeba opens and closes and the heart expands and contracts, human evolution goes through phases in which it flourishes and declines. These phases are dictated by the earth's axis in the northern sky.

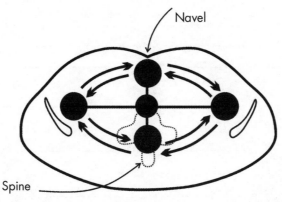

BELT AND THRUSTING CHANNELS AT THE LEVEL OF THE NAVEL (LOWER TAN TIEN)
These energy channels run throughout the body and are interconnected
by horizontal, circular energy bridges.

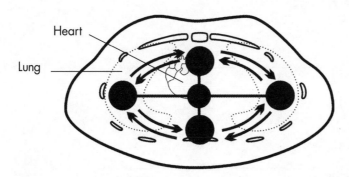

BELT AND THRUSTING CHANNELS AT THE LEVEL OF THE HEART (MIDDLE TAN TIEN)

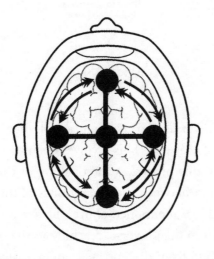

BELT AND THRUSTING CHANNELS AT THE LEVEL OF THE CROWN (UPPER TAN TIEN)

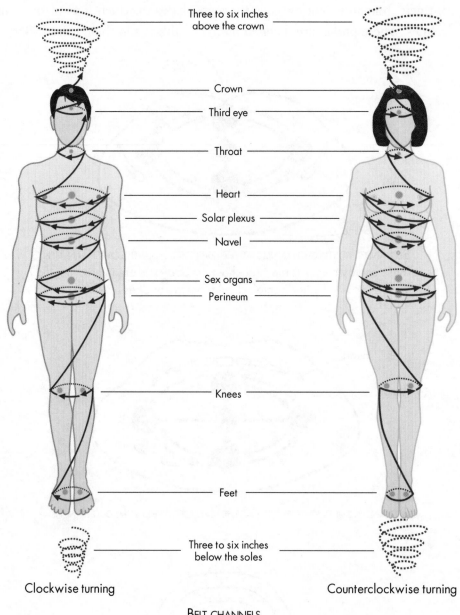

Three to six inches
above the crown

Crown

Third eye

Throat

Heart

Solar plexus

Navel

Sex organs

Perineum

Knees

Feet

Three to six inches
below the soles

Clockwise turning

Counterclockwise turning

BELT CHANNELS

Practicing the Universal Tao techniques will align you with the unique energy situation in the universe. This involves opening several spiritual channels. The first step in this process is the opening of the Microcosmic Orbit (MCO), the connection between the energy lines of the governing and conception vessels, which we mentioned above. This is a channel directly connected to all the orbits in the universe, reaching to the source. If this channel is open, the information from the universe can be easily picked up and integrated. As you can see in the illustration on page 78, there are many different points on the MCO that need to be opened and connected.

These points are directly connected with the Tan Tiens (front and back) and with the points where the Tan Tiens are connected with each other and with the environment. As that same illustration shows, the MCO points, the Tan Tiens, and the *chakras* (as they are known in the Hindu tradition) actually have the same location.

When the MCO opens and connects with the Tan Tiens, the thrusting channels will also start to open up. This enhances the heaven/earth connection, and energizes and detoxifies the body. Then all the five channels (the front and back channels and the three thrusting channels) connect with the belt channels. These are horizontal, circular channels that conserve and protect your life force. When these channels are open and connected, your energy level and your healing capacity will greatly increase. The belt channels connect the conception/governing vessels and the left and right thrusting channels.

By activating the Tan Tiens and fusing the energy into one concentrated "pearl" in the lower Tan Tien, the dualistic experience of time in past and future diminishes and finally dissolves into one infinite experience of now.

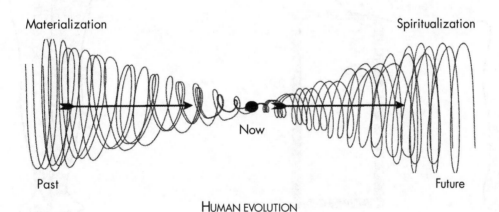

Materialization   Spiritualization

Now

Past   Future

HUMAN EVOLUTION

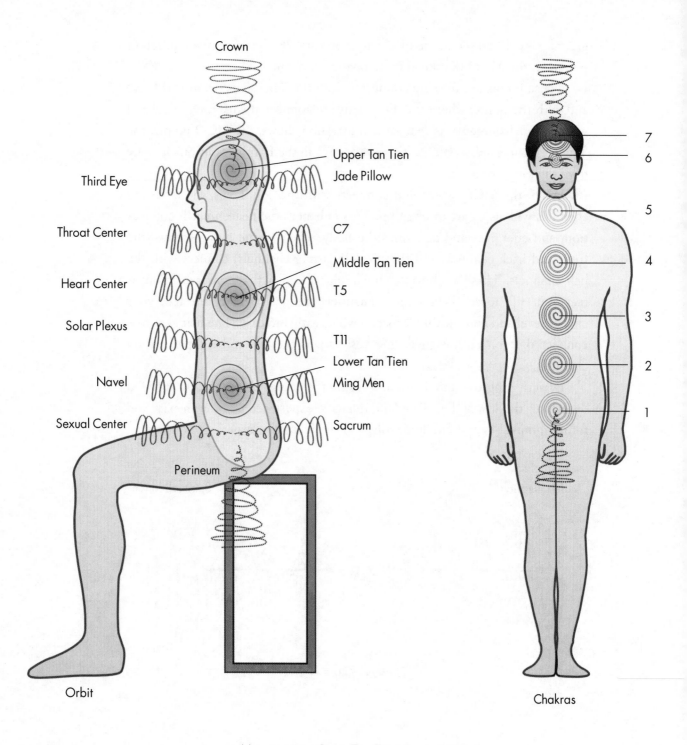

Crown

Upper Tan Tien
Jade Pillow

Third Eye

Throat Center — C7

Middle Tan Tien

Heart Center — T5

Solar Plexus — T11

Lower Tan Tien

Navel — Ming Men

Sexual Center — Sacrum

Perineum

Orbit

Chakras

7
6
5
4
3
2
1

MICROCOSMIC ORBIT, TAN TIENS, AND *CHAKRAS*

Taoist Star
Practices and
Their Effect
on Human
Awareness

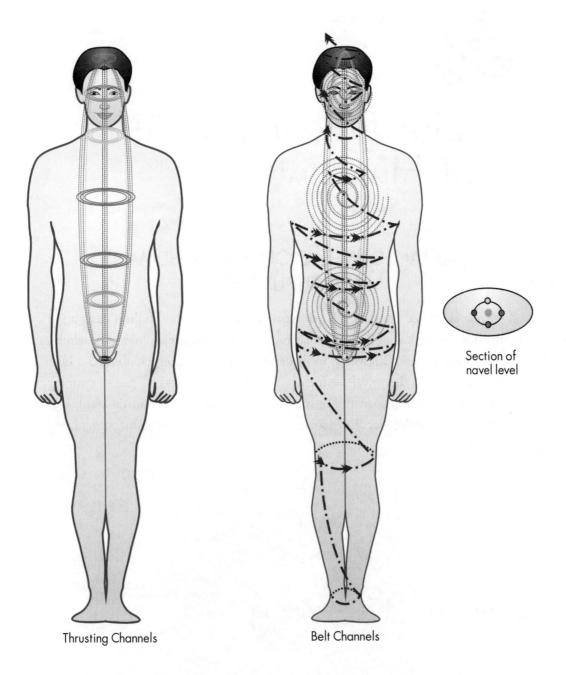

Thrusting Channels

Belt Channels

Section of
navel level

MICROCOSMIC ORBIT, TAN TIENS, THRUSTING CHANNELS, AND BELT CHANNELS

The Development of Humanity

SIMULTANEOUS DEVELOPMENT OF HUMANITY AND THE UNIVERSE

Our planet started its materialization process about 4.5 to 5 billion years ago. After the formation of a dense core and a protective atmosphere, the whole planet was covered with water. In this ancient sea, life emerged about 3.2 billion years ago, in the primitive forms of viruses and bacteria. This, of course, is not when life began in the universe. We, in our true immortal state, are pure life and intelligence. But around that time we began to manifest in physical existence.

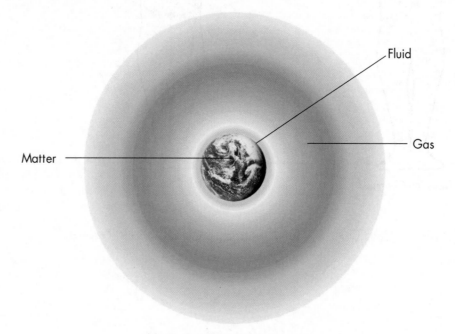

Fluid

Gas

Matter

MATERIALIZATION OF PLANET EARTH

The intelligence that materializes/manifests in the visible world and dematerializes/disappears in other dimensions is one and the same. When the solar system and the Milky Way developed further and became more structured, life on earth began to develop as well. According to Taoist belief, the formation of the solar system and humanity is due to a contracting/materializing force or spiral. This spiral "crystallizes" energetic laws and Chi, causing the formation of our solar system and the earth. The unique atmosphere of Earth has promoted life, with humanity as its highest manifestation.

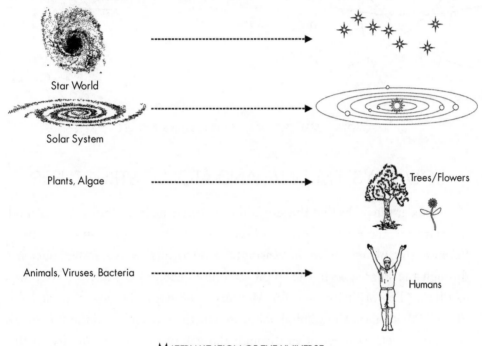

MATERIALIZATION OF THE UNIVERSE

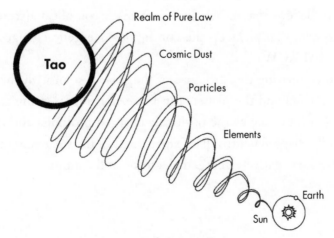

HUMANITY'S MATERIALIZING PROCESS

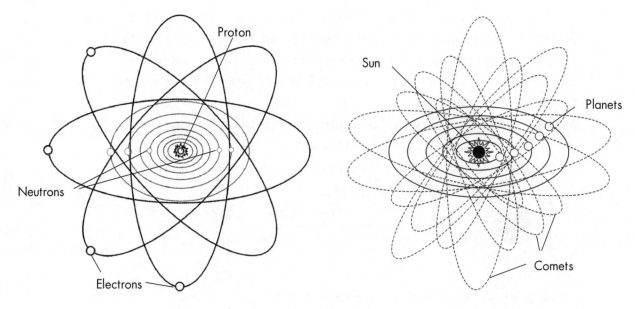

ATOMIC STRUCTURE AND SOLAR SYSTEM STRUCTURE

SOLAR SYSTEM, DNA, AND ATOMIC STRUCTURES

If we look at the paths that the sun and the planets make as they move around the center of the Milky Way, we observe a very interesting spiral structure. Because the planets have increasingly wide orbits as we move outward through the solar system, the spiral structure becomes larger from Mercury to Pluto. (The orbital period for Mercury is 88 days; the orbital period for Pluto is 90,465 days.) The spiral delineated by the movement of the sun, planets, and comets as they move through the galaxy shows a similarity to the structure of atoms, as well as to the structure of DNA.

DNA is the fundamental building block of all living cells. Many Taoist astrologers believe that DNA also contains a complicated transmitter and receiver system that picks up the continuous energetic changes in the solar system and Milky Way.

When comparing the structure of the solar system with the structure of an atom, the sun and the planets can be seen as representing the nucleus of the atom (with the sun as the positively charged proton[s] and the planets as the neutrally charged neutron[s]). The comets of the solar system can be compared with the negatively charged electrons of the atom.

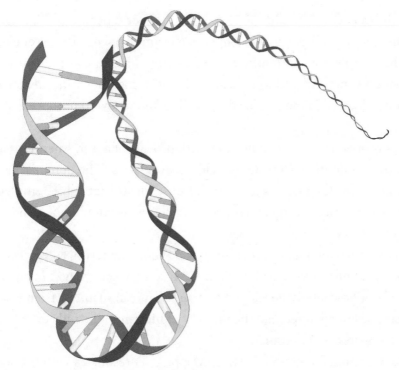

DNA DOUBLE HELIX

ENERGETIC EMBRYOLOGY

The original unity of man and woman is symbolically represented by the Tai Chi (ying/yang) symbol, in which the yin and yang are in perfect balance together within a circle of oneness. The condition prior to the state of duality is the state in which there is only one, indistinguishable unity: the *Wu Chi* state. The energy of man and woman originate from this oneness. This state is still deeply inherent in all of our body cells. Before the egg and sperm physically fuse, man and woman are united on a vibrational level. The original oneness literally draws the egg and sperm together.

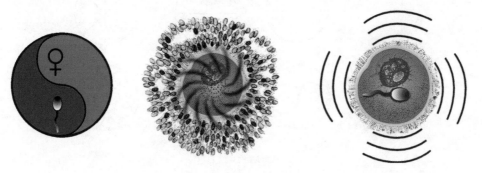

EGG AND SPERM, THE UNIVERSAL BIG BANG, AND THE LITTLE BANG

At the moment of fertilization, or when the sperm penetrates through the egg's membrane wall, a miniature light explosion happens. This event represents the complete evolutionary process of the universe and humanity. The information contained within the egg and sperm, together with the universal consciousness, enable the fertilized egg cell to know how to produce a human being.

This process is very much like the birth process of a star. Energy, gas, and cosmic dust build up in the energy field between stars. The potential rises to a peak and the cloud of cosmic gas and dust divides into different "eggs." Through increasing density and pressure a nuclear reaction ignites, and a new star comes into existence.

The creative intelligence present in the zygote, or fertilized egg cell, can only be called miraculous. Although modern science can analyze many of the details about how a fully developed human infant can manifest from this one cell, many scientists agree that the mystery of life cannot be fully explained by chemistry, genes, and chromosomes.

The vibrational potential between the parents resonates with the soul of the future child, which is present and interactive long before conception. (The soul is believed to enter the embryo around the forty-ninth day after fertilization.) Immediately after fertilization, the zygote divides into two cells of nearly equal size. The process is repeated again and again, so that the two cells are succeeded by four, eight, sixteen, and so on, resulting in a mass of cells known as the *morula*. In this process, new "axes" are created.

The developing fertilized egg, called a *blastocyst* at this stage, stores much of its information in the space and charge between its inside and outside layers, the endoderm and the ectoderm. The inside is related to the woman's

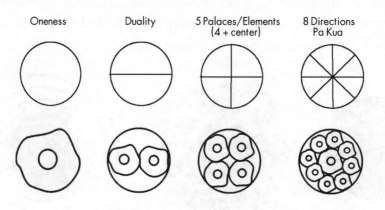

DIVIDING EGG CELL
One gives rise to two, two gives rise to four, four gives rise to eight.

energy and the conception vessel energy. The outside holds the father's energy and the governing vessel energy.

Until day sixteen, the embryo consists of two layers (endoderm and ectoderm). Around this time a third layer, called the mesoderm, materializes along the central axis of the embryo. The *Chong Mo* (the invisible, central axis of the embryo) has been there all the time, but not in a manifested form. The *Chong Mo* creates the connection between the Jing (sexual essence) and the Shen (spiritual energy) of the embryo.

The governing vessel within the mother functions as a "receiving station" that picks up all external vibrations. The conception vessel of the mother internalizes the information and acts as an internal transmission system.

In later development the male energy stays more in the vibrational field and gathers around the developing nervous system and governing vessel of the embryo. The female energy gathers through the developing blood production system in the belly, organs, and the conception vessel of the embryo. The governing vessel is seen as the source of yang energy, the conception vessel as the source of yin energy.

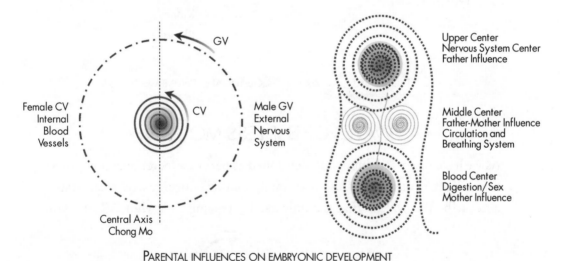

PARENTAL INFLUENCES ON EMBRYONIC DEVELOPMENT

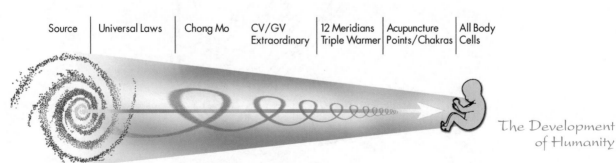

The Development of Humanity

EXTRAORDINARY VESSELS

From the three-layer embryo, the five different elements arise (see chart below). The fire element is divided into two parts (primary and secondary). Thus, six meridian couples are formed. This meridian network spreads throughout the body, with over a thousand vital points where electromagnetic force gathers.

> Ectoderm	Secondary Fire	Triple Warmer
		Pericardium
	Metal	Large Intestine
		Lungs
> Mesoderm	Earth	Spleen
		Stomach
	Wood	Liver
		Gallbladder
> Endoderm	Primary Fire	Heart
		Small Intestine
	Water	Kidneys
		Bladder

EMBRYONIC CELLS, SIX MERIDIANS COUPLES, AND TWELVE MERIDIANS

WAVES OF ENDLESS MOTION

As we have discussed, humanity developed as part of a materialization process that simultaneously manifested throughout the entire galaxy, solar system, and earth. We can say that the universe is evolving as a whole. At the same

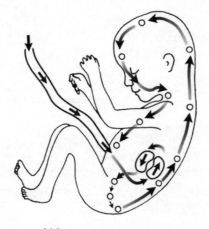

WAVES OF ENDLESS CREATION

time, this evolution occurs through a cyclic, or "wavelike," motion of life and death, materialization and dematerialization. Stars and solar systems are born and come into existence, and one day will be subject to decline and destruction, leaving behind the material that eventually will become new stars. Taoists believe that human civilization likewise has been through cycles of development. Many facts suggest that there must have been highly developed civilizations over five thousand years ago, and Egyptian, Mayan, Tibetan, and Hindu cultures speak of ancient civilizations dating long before recorded history.

The materialistic, Newtonian, rational worldview, which identifies only with our external senses, prevents us from seeing the authenticity of our true origin. When we operate from this perspective, we block ourselves, and we only experience life within physical boundaries, denying the limitless nature of life. Yet we can use our innate wisdom, life experience, and inner intelligence to penetrate deep beyond the limits of the external senses. As illustrated below, all life comes out of the timeless and formless void, the source. The play and interaction of polarity creates waves that differentiate in time and space throughout the physical universe—in the Milky Way, the solar system, the earth, and the body with all its cells, particles, and waves. The deeper we go into our physical existence, the lower the vibration. Freedom lies in the experience of all these different vibrations while relating to the one timeless and spaceless reality.

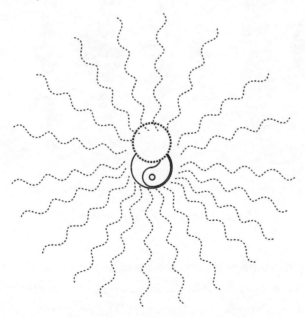

SUN EXPRESSING COSMIC LAW AND CHI

PLANETARY ENERGIES AND HUMAN DEVELOPMENT

The work of Rudolf Steiner, the founder of anthroposophy, examines many interesting connections between planetary energies and human development. While anthroposophy is more closely related to Greek philosophy than to Chinese philosophy, it describes an interesting link between the universe and human development. Greek astrology places its own qualities on the planets, as does Taoist and Chinese astrology. Yet both traditions view the planets as the purest symbols of the personality and emotional/social human behaviors. The planetary world is the world of the soul, with the sun as the middle point or the core of the field of consciousness.

For many centuries in the West, astronomy was based on the Ptolemaic view of the solar system. Ptolemy was a second-century Greek astronomer who described the earth as the unmoving center of the universe, which all planets circled around. (This is seemingly true, of course, from the standpoint of the observer.) In anthroposophy, this Ptolemaic point of view is still used as a map to describe the evolution of the soul.

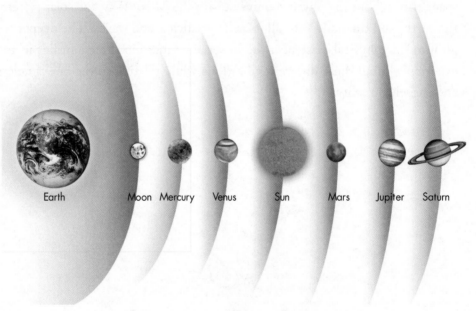

Earth   Moon Mercury   Venus   Sun   Mars   Jupiter Saturn

SOLAR SYSTEM ACCORDING TO PTOLEMY

According to anthroposophy, the earth is the physical place where the human soul connects with the body. Earth, sun, and moon provide the basic energies for the development of humanity. The deep contents of these energies rise when they interact with one another. The meeting of sun and moon

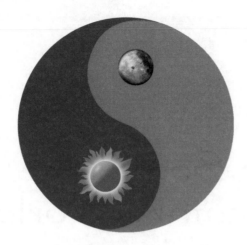

SUN AND MOON

represents the interaction between consciousness and unconsciousness. On another level, sun and moon represent consciousness of mind (sun) and consciousness of body (moon).

Mercury represents the ability to connect on a neutral, nonemotional basis. It connects the energy of sun and moon. Among primitive tribes, the group functions as a unit and is more important than the individual. Connection—the quality of Mercury—gives birth to the Venus quality, which has safety and security as its key attributes. Safety and security are the unconscious goals of forming a group. People gradually learned to increase their survival rate and enhance their security through control of the environment (through agriculture and hunting).

Mars represents the desire to be independent. It stands for the formation of the conscious ego. This is a reaction to the contractile energy of the group. To create balance between the expanding energy of Mars and contractile force of Mercury and Venus, another energy was needed. This energy was found in the gods, through rituals and prayers (religion). This quality is related to Jupiter, which facilitated a deeper and higher unity within the group as well as a growing individual consciousness.

The internal/external struggle in the search for balance and growing consciousness is related to Saturn. Saturn represents the process of decision-making based on one's experiences of pleasure and pain.

The discovery of the three trans-Saturnal planets created an extra dimension or a higher octave in our solar system's human awareness. Thus, anthroposophy provides another model whereby we can understand the coevolution of the solar system and humanity.

The Soul in the Planetary World

The solar system is an energy structure composed of a central area largely consisting of mass and light and nine planetary "awareness" belts encircling its center. The planets are the materialized forms of these awareness belts. Each of these belts has unique frequencies and qualities. The soul remains strongly connected to the sun, and throughout life evolves in expanded awareness through the influence of the successive awareness belts.

Taoist masters clearly distinguish two forms or aspects of the soul: the sun-related cloud soul *(hun)*, and the moon-related white soul *(p'o)*. The *p'o* is the yin aspect, which has seven parts or stages and arises at the time of conception. The *hun*, or yang aspect, joins to the *p'o* at the moment of birth. The *hun* is also seen as the aspect of the soul that rises to heaven at death, whereas the seven *p'o* are the aspects of the soul that return to the earth at death. In the following pages we will not use this dualistic principle of the soul, but rather will see the soul as one.

PROCESS OF INCARNATION AND EXCARNATION

When the soul starts its incarnation process, it moves through the world of stars and is attracted by our solar system, with the sun as its medium. The sun functions as a giant satellite station between the worlds of stars and planets.

According to the karmic information carried by the soul, it will remain a shorter or longer period within the "frequency" or influence of some planets. During these periods it receives the necessary information to create or awaken specific learning possibilities. The fact that each soul remains longer in one sphere of influence than another creates very distinctive qualities in the character of each person. We have stronger connections to some planets and weaker connections to others.

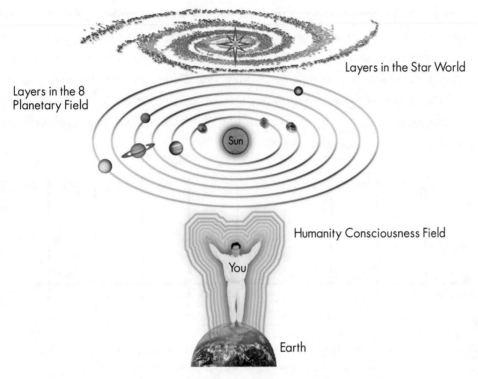

Layers in the Star World

Layers in the 8 Planetary Field

Sun

Humanity Consciousness Field

You

Earth

STAR WORLD, PLANETARY WORLD, AND HUMAN AWARENESS FIELD

During the incarnation process the soul will move from the unmanifested world through the star world, the planets, and the moon-earth sphere, constantly attracted by the force of the sun, and later, the earth. The electro-plasmic force of humanity around the earth functions as an awareness belt that connects the soul with life on earth.

When a baby is born, the incarnation process is not yet complete, as we can clearly see in the personality of the child. In the first two seven-year life

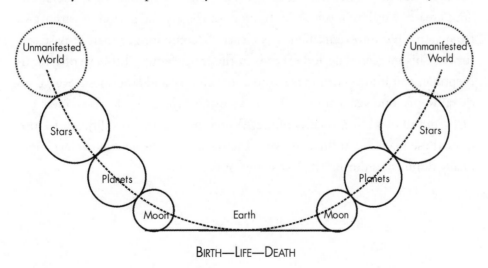

Unmanifested World

Unmanifested World

Stars

Stars

Planets

Planets

Moon

Earth

Moon

BIRTH—LIFE—DEATH

cycles, the full incarnation of the soul still has to be completed. Often around puberty, at the beginning of the third stage, the true personality reveals itself, sometimes as a shock to the parents. The reverse happens in the last cycles of life. The person increasingly loses interest and connection with earth and life on the planet as the soul withdraws toward the higher worlds. Although they are on opposite sides of the spiral of life, children and old people often dwell with their soul in a higher realm.

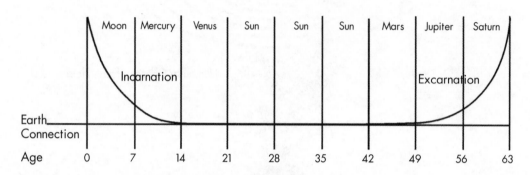

DEVELOPMENT OF THE SOUL THROUGH THE PLANETARY WORLD
BASED ON ANTHROPOSOPHICAL THEORY

In the above illustration, based on the anthroposophical view of the growth of the soul, the sun is seen as the center of soul development. The sun reflects the law of triple unity in the universe. Three planets are placed on each side.

The stages of incomplete incarnation are the developmental stages of the moon and Mercury for children, and of beginning excarnation in the stages of Jupiter and Saturn for older people. The discovery of the three trans-Saturnal planets has occurred together with growing human life expectations. This creates a different schedule. In modern society the period of withdrawal from active life into retirement has clearly become longer than in past centuries. This increased period extends in the trans-Saturnal sphere of Uranus, Neptune, and Pluto. For people with a low energy and awareness level, these extra twenty-one years are simply an extension, which results in an increased life span but of a lower quality of life. When this occurs, it is difficult to integrate these planetary influences, with the result that the awareness level drastically diminishes during the last stages of life.

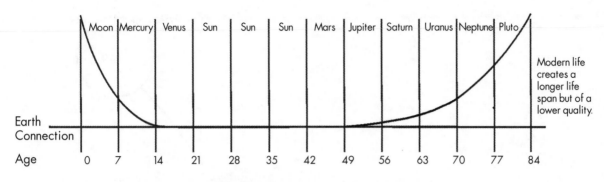

| Moon | Mercury | Venus | Sun | Sun | Sun | Mars | Jupiter | Saturn | Uranus | Neptune | Pluto |

Modern life creates a longer life span but of a lower quality.

Earth Connection

Age   0   7   14   21   28   35   42   49   56   63   70   77   84

MODERN LIFE CREATES A LONGER LIFE SPAN.

APPLICATION IN THE UNIVERSAL TAO PRACTICE

In the Universal Tao practice the period of the sun (ages twenty-one to forty-two years) is used to build up a strong connection with the sun and the North Star consciousness (see illustration, page 94). The North Star is the Taoist spiritual gate. It is often used in advanced meditations as the focal point through which pure universal Chi may be transferred to the human plane and used in Cosmic Healing Chi Kung. This is where we derive the luminous violet color that energizes our body. Once the connection with the source is established through the North Star and the universal light, the effect of the planets on the practitioner's emotional and mental state will be reduced. To establish the sun and North Star connection, the five elemental forces must be balanced and the frequencies of the awareness belts around the sun (related to the planets) must be integrated. During the sun period, the collective consciousness inherent in each cell of our body will be nurtured by the high quality of the sun's frequency. This energy is mostly used to manifest oneself in the world, through relationships, work, home life, children, and so forth.

In Taoist practice the awakening light of the sun period is a perfect time to establish the North Star/spiritual connection. Once the connection with the spiritual realm is established we can distinguish two different realities (spirit and earthbound). The more volatile planetary influences will still affect us, but our rooting to earth and heaven will make it much easier to stay in connection with the spiritual laws, the life force in our body, and their interaction. In this way we stop nurturing the ego and begin to live a life beyond the personality and the related planetary spheres.

Through the Universal Tao practice the sun period can be used to cultivate the soul and spirit body. The soul is the medium between the physical plane and the spiritual world. The soul naturally follows the personality's evolution through the planetary spheres, but the spirit does not have this

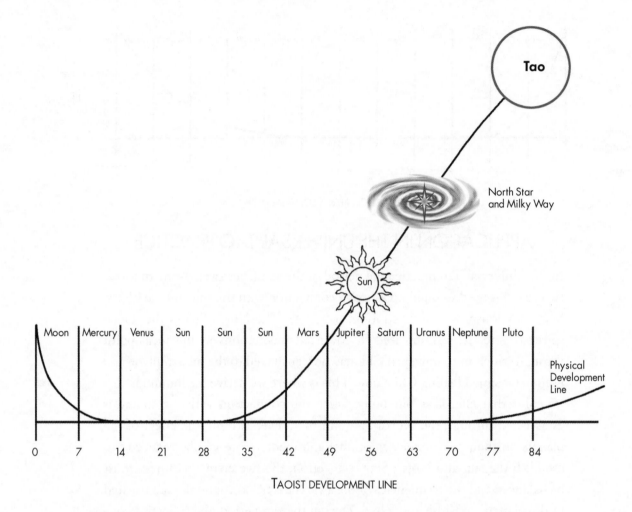

Tao

North Star
and Milky Way

Sun

| Moon | Mercury | Venus | Sun | Sun | Sun | Mars | Jupiter | Saturn | Uranus | Neptune | Pluto |

Physical
Development
Line

0　7　14　21　28　35　42　49　56　63　70　77　84

TAOIST DEVELOPMENT LINE

limitation. An important factor in our development is our level of realization and point of identification: we can identify primarily with our finite personalities or with our unlimited spiritual nature. The sun period is also the time when the level of Chi in the physical body is at its peak. The physical and biological development is at its peak at around twenty-eight years of age in men and twenty-four years of age in women. At that time the body becomes a temple in which the soul and spirit can be cultivated. Taoist practitioners cultivate quantity of life (life span) combined with quality of life (spiritual realization).

Through the Universal Tao practices, this peak state can be maintained and even improved upon during the following decades. Getting older does not have to mean getting weaker. Many Taoist masters become more fit as they grow older, which has been confirmed by Western doctors. For Taoist practitioners, advancing in years means advancing in experience, intelligence, and wisdom, and integrating greater energy in the body. When the sun and North Star connections are open, your whole life will be inspired and guided by the unlimited wisdom of the universe. The connection with the light will enable you to lead an active but peaceful life. You will still experience the growth of the soul through the more emotional influences of the planetary spheres, but the spiritual connection will allow you to observe this process, see the deeper reality through the ups and downs of emotions, and integrate these energies within the physical body.

In this way the energy of our experiences is integrated to nurture our consciousness. Rudolf Steiner said that the goal in life is to balance the planetary qualities to reach the highest state in the solar system, which he called "the sun awareness." During excarnation, the soul will move again through the planetary world and will be purified from all earthly, materialistic, and emotional experiences. The fruits of the life just completed are harvested and condensed to form the seeds for the next life. This process is continued outside the planetary sphere in the world of stars and the immaterialized realm of vibrations.

In the Universal Tao, the "fusion of the five elements" practice is used to balance the qualities of the five elements in the body. This practice is also called *internal alchemy*. (See the Universal Tao publication *Fusion of the Five Elements* for a detailed explanation of this ancient Taoist practice.) After strengthening and purifying the body through the basic practices and fusion practice, the energy and virtues of the five vital organs (kidney, heart, spleen, lungs, and liver) are cultivated. (See *Taoist Cosmic Healing*, Inner Smile Practice.) These energies are gathered in collection areas (the *pa kua* collection points) around the navel. From these collection points, the energy is blended, purified, and stored in the lower Tan Tien.

Through these practices, the energy is condensed until it becomes a radiating pearl, located at the original meeting point where the information of the first cell and basic spark of the body is kept (in the area of the small intestine). Taoists use the metaphor of the "pearl" or "crystal" to refer to this highly concentrated, purified energy. The pearl is cultivated and slowly transformed into spiritual energy. It becomes the house of the soul and spirit body as well as one's balance, control, and universal connection point.

Once the pearl is cultivated, it can serve to open different energy channels in the body and enable one to travel, via one's consciousness, outside the physical body into the worlds of the planets, stars, and vibrations. The pearl has the same function as the sun in our solar system: centering, collecting, controlling, and connecting to higher realms. When the center is weak (the pearl has not been cultivated), there is no central point of consciousness or

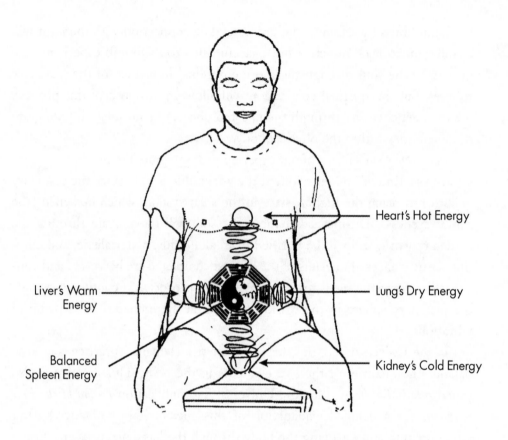

PA KUA COLLECTION POINTS

Heart's Hot Energy

Liver's Warm Energy

Lung's Dry Energy

Balanced Spleen Energy

Kidney's Cold Energy

control. This implies weakness and inability to decide where to go or what to do. When we use the mind to gather the energy at one point, the spark that is still glowing inside us will ignite and start to shine again—just as our sun ignited some 5 billion years ago.

When the pearl is shining and stable in the lower Tan Tien, it becomes the source of energy for all the organs. In Chinese medicine this is the yang meridian of primary fire, the center of transformation.

When the pearl is stronger and more refined, it can be moved upward to

CONTRACTING SPIRAL; ENERGY GATHERING IN THE CENTER; SPONTANEOUS IGNITION

the heart center. While the fire of the small intestine, where the pearl is initially located, is a denser, more physical fire, the fire of the heart carries a higher vibration. This fire is related to the quality of the sun, the soul, and the state of compassion. It is the practitioner's task to create the right internal condition for moving the pearl into the heart center by self-cultivation and good deeds for the benefit of all beings. In the advanced *Kan* and *Li* and "immortal" practices, the pearl moves up to the center of the head. It moves upward by itself as the fruit of self-transformation. At this point the pearl changes and acquires a very high frequency, related to the world of spirit.

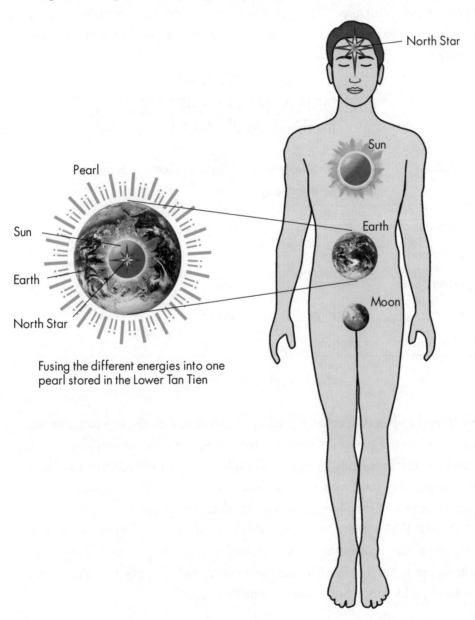

Fusing the different energies into one pearl stored in the Lower Tan Tien

FUSING THE PEARL

During meditation practice it is good to expand one's energy field and connect with all forces of the universe. Concentrating and storing energy in the lower Tan Tien will make these energies available in your daily life. During meditation we can use the moon and earth force in the lower Tan Tien, the sun energy in the middle Tan Tien, and the North Star energy in the upper Tan Tien. When one completes a period of meditation practice it is good to bring the energy of the North Star together with the energy of the sun in the Middle Tan Tien. Then one should bring both of these energies together with the energy of the earth or the lower Tan Tien. This is the "three-in-one principle." This process of gathering and connecting energy symbolizes unification, and represents the spiritual world becoming the core of one's life.

USE OF PLANETARY ENERGIES IN EAST AND WEST

Translation	English Spelling of Chinese Name	Western Name	Element
Chronographic Star	Ch'en Hsing	Mercury	Water
Grand White	T'ai Po	Venus	Metal
Sparkling Diluter	Ying Huo	Mars	Fire
Year Star	Sui Hsing	Jupiter	Wood
Quelling Star	Chen Hsing	Saturn	Earth

FIVE PLANETS AND FIVE ELEMENTS

In China the planets have been used in connection with the five elements and the five heavenly palaces, in their relationship with the twenty-eight lunar mansions, for thousands of years. The planets were called the "naked-eye five" or the "five stars" or sometimes the "five pacers." The translation of the Chinese names of the planets gives us an idea of the nature of their energy.

Outside China there is a long history of the astrological use of planets. The Babylonian civilization made astrological recordings as early as the third millennium B.C.E. The Babylonians also connected the planets with different gods and goddesses, a link found in many cultures.

Planet	Babylonian	Hindu	Egyptian	Greek	Roman
Sun	Shamash	Surya	Ra	Helios	Apollo
Moon	Sin	Chandra	Chamse	Artemis	Diana
Mercury	Nabu	Hanuman	Toth	Hermes	Mercurius
Venus	Ishtar	Lalita	Hathoor	Aphrodite	Venus
Mars	Nergal	Mangala	Horus	Aries	Mars
Jupiter	Marduk	Indra	Amoun	Zeus	Jupiter
Saturn	Ninurta	Brahma	Sebek	Kronos	Saturn

PLANETS LINKED WITH GODS/GODDESSES IN VARIOUS CULTURES

Western astrological symbols are different from, but comparable to, those used in Taoist astrology. Western astrological symbols for the planets have similar connections to the world of soul and spirit. The sun is the image of concentrated spirit.

SUN

The circle is a sign of wholeness; the dot represents the center of the solar system.

MOON

The vertical division of the circle into two half-circles is the symbol for the moon and also for the soul (divided consciousness).

EARTH

The cross represents the integration of matter and spirit.

VENUS
Venus symbolizes spirit over matter.

MARS
Mars shows the cross of matter over spirit.

MERCURY
Mercury is the planet of connection, mediating between the different forces. It also represents the role of spirit as a bridge between soul and body.

JUPITER
Jupiter shows the soul elevated over the cross of matter.

SATURN
Saturn is the cross of matter above the crescent of the soul.

In Greek mythology, observation of the heavenly bodies was seen as the vehicle for getting in contact with the higher psychic world, and different soul and personality types were based on the different energies of the planets. The planets were also associated with specific gods and goddesses, thus identifying some planets as "male" and others as "female." For example, Venus is considered a female planet connected with the Greek goddess of love and beauty, Aphrodite. And Jupiter is known as a male planet connected with the dominating, controlling energy of the god Zeus.

In ancient Taoist astrology, the planets were seen as expressions of the five elements. The energy of the planets was also understood to be related to the colors of the five elements and the seasonal cycle. For example, wood is the element associated with spring. Spring gives birth to new life and is considered female. Wood and spring are associated with Jupiter, and Jupiter is understood to be a female planet. Metal is the element associated with autumn. In autumn, life withdraws and contracts, and is considered male. Metal and autumn are associated with Venus, so it is seen as a male planet.

Because of these different associations, Chinese and Western astrology link different personality types, male/female energies, and body organs with particular planets. So it is important to use the planets according to one system only and not to mix them.

	VENUS		MERCURY		JUPITER		MARS		SATURN	
Modality	- Lungs +		- Kidneys +		- Liver +		- Heart +		- Spleen +	
Emotion	Sadness, Grief	Righteousness, Courage	Fear, Stress, Fright	Gentleness	Anger	Kindness	Impatience, Cruelty, Hate	Love, Honor, Respect	Worry	Fairness, Openness
Shape	Collapsed, Flattened ball	Tall, Straight	Awkward, Tiny, Compressed	Round, Full, Expansive	Spearlike, Sharp	Round, Smooth	Moving, Spiny	Straight, Open	Irregular	Open, Wide, Big
Color	Gray	Bright white	Dark gray, Cloudy	Bright sky blue	Red, Cloudy	Soft green	Orange, Muddy	Bright red	Cloudy	Mellow yellow
Smell	Musty	Pure, Fresh	Foul, Urine	Fresh	Pungent	Sweet, Fragrant	Sharp, Burnt	Aromatic Incense	Sour	Clean, Dry
Temperature	Cold	Comfortable, Warm	Cold, Chilly	Cool, Comfortable	Hot, Explosive	Warm, Pleasant	Unsteady	Warm, Full	Humid	Warm, Mid-range
Sound	Low, No force	Strong, Firm, Resonant	High-pitched, Shrill	Whisper, Pleasant to ear	Flashing, Loud	Melodious	Noisy, Irregular	Deep, Stable, Steady, Solid	Shaky	Clear, Soft, In tune
Feeling	No energy, Exhausted	Uplifted	Tight, Closed in	Relaxed, High, Centered	Pain, Tough, Rough	Nurtured	Irregular	Stable, Protected	Uncertain	Balanced, Even
Texture	Crumpled	Firm but comfortable	Slippery	Velvet	Rough	Soft	Cactuslike	Comfortable, Secure	Sticky	Smooth, Firm
Size	Deflated, Low	Expanding upward	Small	Limitless	Expanding, Exploding	Expanding gently	Small, Pointed	Expanding	Out of proportion	Big, Deep
Taste	Salty	Satisfying	Salty	Mild, Honey	Bitter	Sweet	Acidic	Satisfying	Sour	Smooth, Clean
Direction	Downward	Upward	Scattered	Circular	Attacking	Enfolding	Scattered	Open, Steady	Constricted	Horizontal

TYPICAL QUALITIES OF THE FIVE VITAL ORGANS IN CHINESE SYSTEM

The Craniosacral System, Elements, Star Palaces, and Planetary Forces

THE DEVELOPMENT OF THE CRANIOSACRAL RHYTHM

Taoist views about the structure of the universe and the invisible world have been partly corroborated by recent discoveries in science. These discoveries make the Taoist esoteric knowledge, particularly the health treatments, seem more pragmatic.

Traditional Taoist teachings note that the power of the governing vessel (the important energy channel that brings energy up the back of the body) is controlled by the power of its two poles: the sacrum and the cranium. The governing vessel is a channel for energy that comes all the way from the Tao, and a free flow of energy between the two poles is essential to provide the body with the right information to function in accordance with universal law. The treatment of the physical manifestation of this system has been developed in a specialized form of bodywork, deriving from osteopathy, called *craniosacral therapy*.

The governing vessel has been used as a spiritual channel for more than five thousand years, but the art of craniosacral therapy is only about a hundred years old and focuses on other energies in the human skull. The discovery of the forms of bodily intelligence that are used in craniosacral therapy appear to be directly connected with universal and human evolution. It is a further development of awareness and sensitivity of the bioplasmic field (one's personal aura) and the electroplasmic field (which is shared with all other humans).

Long ago humans were only aware of their rhythm of breathing. Primitive human beings recognized the breath as a sign of life. They were strongly physically dependent and physically oriented. The breath provided them with vital energy (cosmic light) and oxygen for nourishment. The heart center was undeveloped, and they were not aware of their heartbeat. The development of the heart center gave birth to a more conscious soul connection. As the consciousness of breathing developed and grew into the heart center, the sociability of the lung energy came forward.

In the heart center, the connection with other beings, the emotions, and the virtues arises. When the heart center developed into a higher state, compassion evolved as a bridge to the higher mental and spiritual levels. Chi and awareness in the nervous system are known in every spiritual tradition, but the rhythm of the craniosacral system is a relatively new discovery.

System	Level	Connection
Meridian rhythm (cycle)	Spiritual	Unmanifested world
Cranial rhythm	Higher mental/spiritual	Star connection
Heart rhythm	Lower mental/social/emotional	Sun connection
Breathing rhythm	Physical	Earth/Moon connection

DEVELOPMENT OF RHYTHM SYSTEMS

THE CRANIOSACRAL SYSTEM

The craniosacral rhythm develops through the subtle cranial shifts that occur during the unfolding of the embryonic nervous system. It also can be seen as a translation of the information in the governing vessel. The brain and its ventricles produce a liquid called cerebrospinal fluid. This fluid is rhythmically pumped into the subarachnoid space between the layers of the meninges, the three membranous layers of connective tissue that envelop the brain and spinal cord. The outermost layer of the meninges, or dura mater, is extremely tough and is fused with the membranous lining of the skull. The thin arachnoid membrane lies below and in close contact with the dura mater. The innermost layer, or pia mater, is in direct contact with the brain and spinal cord and contains the blood vessels that supply them. The pia mater and arachnoid membrane are separated by the subarachnoid space containing the cerebrospinal fluid.

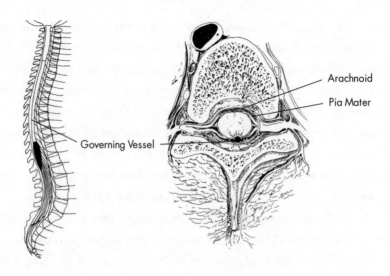

Arachnoid

Pia Mater

Governing Vessel

THE MENINGAL SYSTEM CONTAINS THE ENERGY OF THE GOVERNING VESSEL.

The governing vessel is located along the back of the spinal cord, in the subarachnoid space between the arachnoid membrane and pia mater. In this way the governing vessel is constantly charging the cerebrospinal fluid and the spine.

The cerebrospinal fluid is produced in the ventricles of the brain and is completely renewed every five to six hours. There are about 135 cubic centimeters of this fluid present in the body, and the ventricles secrete more than half a liter daily. It must circulate continuously. In addition to the spiritual information from the governing vessel, the cerebrospinal fluid contains the deep memory of biological evolution from the oldest planetary oceans. The record of more than 3 billion years of evolution from bacteria and viruses to human beings is stored there. The fluid in the system cycles at a rate of about eight to twelve times per minute. During the phases the membrane system in the head contracts and expands, causing the movement of cerebrospinal fluid in the spine. The cranial "waves" range from 0.04 to 1.5 millimeters, but with some training they can be felt throughout the whole body. The craniosacral rhythm is fully independent of the breathing process.

Universal Law	Spirit	
Aura Awareness Field Chakras/Meridians	Chi	3 Realms
Spinal Fluid Cranial Bones	Matter	

THREE REALMS IN THE UNIVERSE AND IN THE HUMAN BODY

Even though the energy in the cranial system is more spiritually oriented, four different dimensions can be recognized (spiritual, mental, emotional, and physical). Any kind of impact on one of these four dimensions changes the quality and energy in the other three.

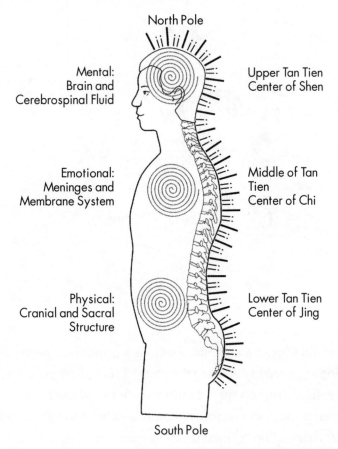

North Pole

Mental:
Brain and
Cerebrospinal Fluid

Upper Tan Tien
Center of Shen

Emotional:
Meninges and
Membrane System

Middle of Tan
Tien
Center of Chi

Physical:
Cranial and Sacral
Structure

Lower Tan Tien
Center of Jing

South Pole

SPIRITUAL GOVERNING VESSEL AND ITS AWARE EXPRESSION (CRANIOSACRAL SYSTEM)

The whole craniosacral system is a big antenna and transmitter of information to all the different energy levels in the body. To work with it, it is necessary to practice, to feel and study the different layers of the system. The physical layer (cranial and spinal bones) and the spiritual layer (governing vessel) are the most easy and most practical ones to register in the body. Working with the cerebrospinal fluid and emotional meninges requires more study and practice. The craniosacral system has a north pole (the cranium) and a south pole (the sacrum). Under normal conditions they work together in perfect rhythm. The cranium is the pneumatic/mechanical driving force; the sacrum follows the cranium impulses. In cases of stress or blockages there can be small timing differences between the two.

The Craniosacral
System,
Elements, Star
Palaces, and
Planetary Forces

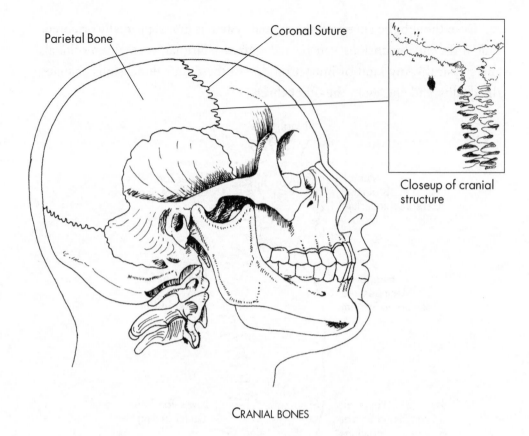

Parietal Bone   Coronal Suture

Closeup of cranial
structure

CRANIAL BONES

The suture lines in the cranium form zigzag, pointed protrusions that
have a function in receiving stellar vibrations. From these structures subtle
energy/information channels spread out through the whole body.

To understand the craniosacral system, it is helpful to look at some simple anatomical charts. The "cranial bowl" contains ten major external bones,
five of which are used in Universal Tao meditations.

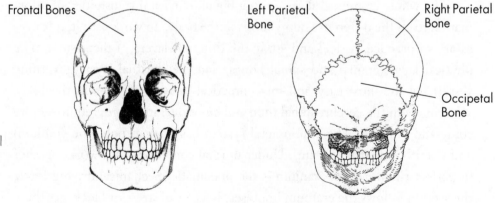

Frontal Bones   Left Parietal Bone   Right Parietal Bone

Occipetal Bone

FRONT AND REAR VIEWS OF HUMAN SKULL

The Craniosacral
System,
Elements, Star
Palaces, and
Planetary Forces

106

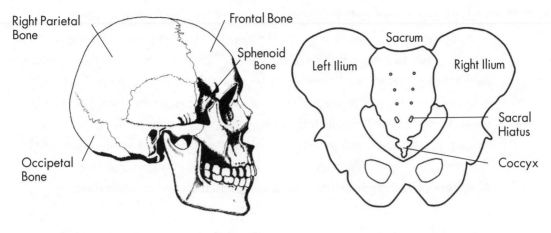

CRANIOSACRAL SYSTEM

The craniosacral system has high and low "tides" according to the movement of the cranial bones and membranes. Each individual bone has a very specific movement. In addition, each bone bends subtly, like a piece of hard rubber. We can also see a general movement of the cranium as a whole. In the "flexion stage" the cranium becomes wider and shorter. In the "extension stage" the skull becomes narrower and longer. You can compare it with a balloon you hold on both sides. If you softly press and release every six to seven seconds, you get an effect similar to the cranium during flexion/extension. The bones of the sacrum also move in conjunction with the flexion and extension of the cranium.

Many therapists now work with various types of craniosacral therapy. In the last twenty years craniosacral therapy has evolved into a very effective form of bodywork that can help create balance, release blockages, and energize the body. Most of these therapists work with the bones, membranes, meninges, and cerebrospinal fluid. Some therapists work with the craniosacral system as a separate unit of the body or as the only important system in the body, which is an incomplete approach.

Universal laws organize all the systems and energies of the body. Working

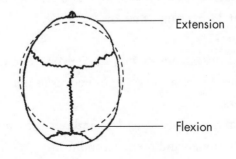

CRANIAL FLEXION AND EXTENSION

with planetary and stellar energies brings an important dimension to craniosacral therapy because it helps to get closer to the origin of the system and how it relates to universal principles. The Universal Tao practices that involve stellar and planetary meditations can be very valuable in deepening the consciousness and understanding of healers and bodyworkers. Balancing the planet and star energies will result in deep, long-lasting changes in the lives of both healing practitioners and patients. When the energies are balanced, universal information naturally reaches us in a more harmonious way, and many of the blockages on the physical, emotional, and mental levels gradually dissolve.

THE FIVE ELEMENTS, FIVE STAR PALACES, FIVE PLANETS, AND FIVE CRANIAL BONES

The five planets are the physical representations of the different awareness layers in the solar system. They are also a materialized form of the law of the five elements. The law of the five elements is an important principle in ancient and modern Chinese society. It is used in medicine, astrology, politics, and a variety of other fields.

Some Taoist meditation practices link the planets with the cranial bones. Others make connections between the stars and the sutures between the cranial bones. One Taoist practice places the planet Saturn in the heart, Mars above the head, Mercury under the feet, Venus in the right palm, and Jupiter in the left palm. In the Universal Tao practice, we see the cranial system as our own compact representation of the five planets (the central part of the solar system) and the five star palaces (the five regions of the heavens defined by projecting the four directions and the center into the sky). The five main cranial bones are in direct connection with the energies of the planets, stars, and elements, and react directly on all information coming through this channel. From the cranial bowl, the energy moves down into the organs and different body systems.

Awareness of the cranial system and its connection to the planetary, stellar, elemental forces helps us to:

- Create a direct contact with the universe and its enormous energy source.
- Gain insight in our karmic influences as determined by various planets and stars.
- Develop the ability to understand our present lives, reactions, and physical, emotional, and mental condition.
- Stabilize and integrate these various energies.

The Craniosacral
System,
Elements, Star
Palaces, and
Planetary Forces

108

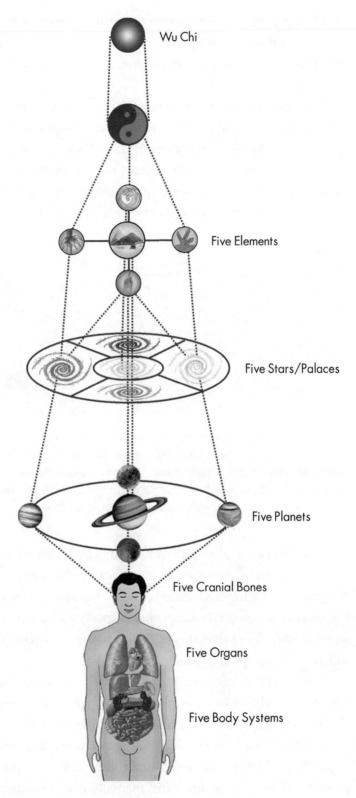

Wu Chi

Five Elements

Five Stars/Palaces

Five Planets

Five Cranial Bones

Five Organs

Five Body Systems

FIVE ELEMENTS, PALACES, PLANETS, CRANIAL BONES

The Craniosacral
System,
Elements, Star
Palaces, and
Planetary Forces

Once a clear connection with the planets is established, the stellar/galactic energies from the five palaces can be integrated. With continued practice, direct contact with the law of the five elements in the vibrational world can be achieved.

The bone structure is our most dense body system. The crystalline and mineral structure of the bones has (besides its supportive function) a primary role in attracting high energy frequencies. Also, the hormonal activities in the glands in the head have an important role. Both the hormones and mineral structures are very condensed substances that have the ability to attract the extremely high vibrations of spiritual energies and star frequencies.

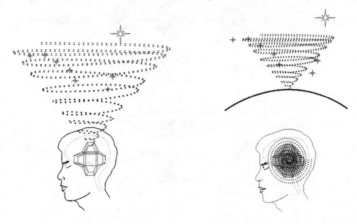

OPEN AND CLOSED CRYSTAL ROOM

When the crystal room is open, there is a connection to the universe. When the crystal room is closed—due to too much mental activity, stress, low energy, and negative emotions—there is no universal connection.

The glands serve as transmitters and transformers of the subtle (high) energy frequencies, which can then enter into the organs and the layers of the body that have a lower vibration. These channels can only be experienced in the silence of the empty spaces between the turbulent activity of emotions and thoughts. The planetary and stellar connection generally depends on two different factors: prenatal and postnatal.

The prenatal influence is the karmic information we carry into each incarnation. This is based on the tasks and messages the soul receives during the incarnation process, according to the sum of past life experiences.

The postnatal influence is the physical, emotional, and mental conditions of our life, which greatly affect our ability to receive information from the universe. If we get too busy and mentally overactive, stress gathers in our body and we feel increasingly separated from ourselves and from life. This condition makes it impossible to take in information from the universe.

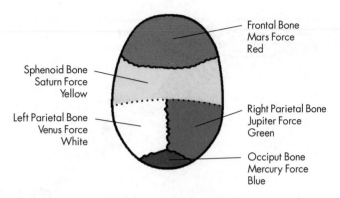

Frontal Bone
Mars Force
Red

Sphenoid Bone
Saturn Force
Yellow

Left Parietal Bone
Venus Force
White

Right Parietal Bone
Jupiter Force
Green

Occiput Bone
Mercury Force
Blue

TOP VIEW OF THE CRANIUM

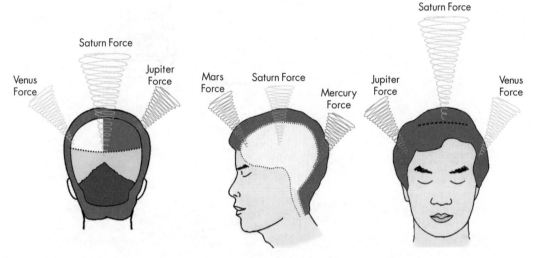

Saturn Force

Venus Force

Jupiter Force

Mars Force

Saturn Force

Mercury Force

Jupiter Force

Saturn Force

Venus Force

BACK VIEW, LEFT SIDE, AND FRONT SIDE OF THE CRANIUM, WITH ASSOCIATED PLANET FORCES

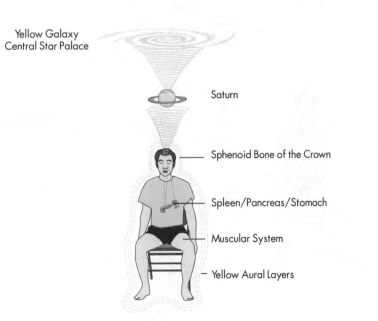

Yellow Galaxy
Central Star Palace

Saturn

Sphenoid Bone of the Crown

Spleen/Pancreas/Stomach

Muscular System

Yellow Aural Layers

EARTH ELEMENT

The Craniosacral
System,
Elements, Star
Palaces, and
Planetary Forces

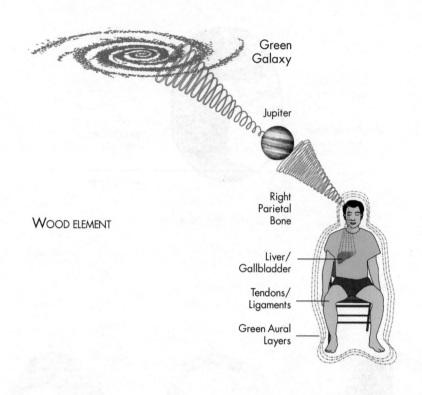

Green
Galaxy

Jupiter

WOOD ELEMENT

Right
Parietal
Bone

Liver/
Gallbladder

Tendons/
Ligaments

Green Aural
Layers

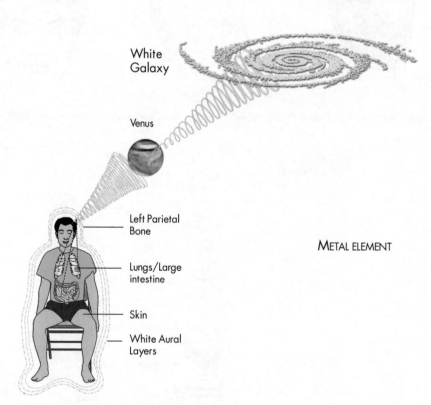

White
Galaxy

Venus

Left Parietal
Bone

METAL ELEMENT

Lungs/Large
intestine

Skin

White Aural
Layers

The Craniosacral
System,
Elements, Star
Palaces, and
Planetary Forces

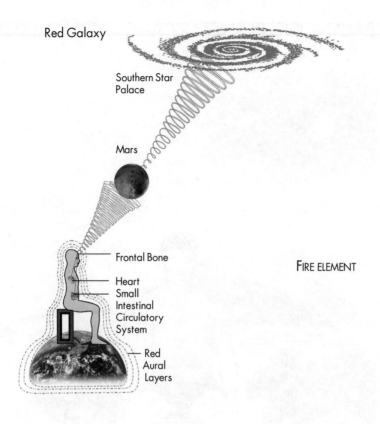

Red Galaxy

Southern Star
Palace

Mars

FIRE ELEMENT

Frontal Bone

Heart
Small
Intestinal
Circulatory
System

Red
Aural
Layers

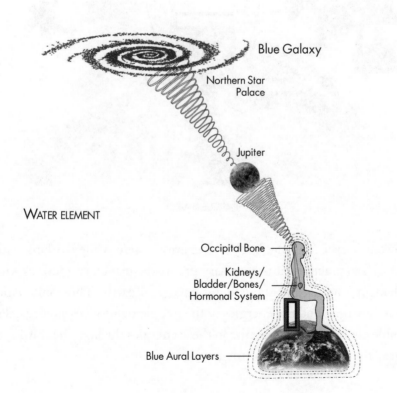

Blue Galaxy

Northern Star
Palace

Jupiter

WATER ELEMENT

Occipital Bone

Kidneys/
Bladder/Bones/
Hormonal System

Blue Aural Layers

The Craniosacral
System,
Elements, Star
Palaces, and
Planetary Forces

BALANCING PLANETARY AND EARTH ENERGIES

INNER BALANCE

To prevent overheating the body and energy system while working with the Universal Tao practices, it is necessary to mix the planetary energies with the five elemental forces and the cooling energy of earth. The combination of planetary energies and the energies of the five elements gives a more balanced and stable energy. We can breathe in these energies through the third eye, the skin near the related organ, or the navel.

The Craniosacral
System,
Elements, Star
Palaces, and
Planetary Forces

114

Earthly Connections for the Planetary Energies

Jupiter	Liver	Tree/Wood energy	Green
Mars	Heart	Fire/Flame energy	Red
Saturn	Spleen	Earth/Soil energy	Yellow
Venus	Lungs	Lake/Metal energy	White
Mercury	Kidneys	Water/River energy	Blue

The energies of the wind, sky, thunder, lightning, lakes, and flowers are also very useful. All natural energies are a direct source of cosmic energy for us.

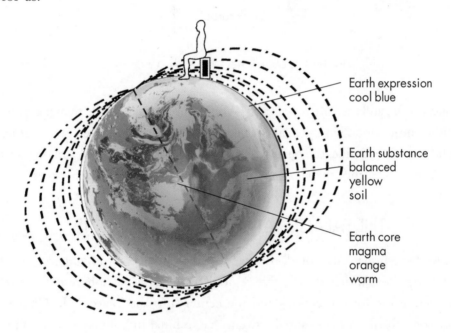

Earth expression
cool blue

Earth substance
balanced
yellow
soil

Earth core
magma
orange
warm

THREE ASPECTS OF THE EARTH FORCE

The planet earth has three different energies. The different layers of the planet have different energetic qualities and colors. If we tune in to the surface of the earth, we connect to the earth/soil quality, which is yellow. If we tune in to the energy radiated by the earth's centrifugal force, we perceive a cool, blue energy. If we go deeper into the earth, we can perceive a warm, orange/red energy, which is related to the earth's core.

The energy of the inner earth relates more to the female quality while the energy of the surface of the earth relates more to the male quality. According to traditional Taoist teachings, women are more yin in their overall energetic

The Craniosacral System, Elements, Star Palaces, and Planetary Forces

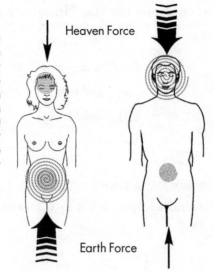

More earth force influence, more energy in the lower body; more density/warmth in the Lower Tan Tien (stability of the egg) and softer/cooler on the outside of the body

Heaven Force

More heaven force influence, more energy in upper body; more dense/warm outer layer (energy related to the sperm energy) and softer/cooler on the inside of the body

Earth Force

HEAVEN AND EARTH FORCES IN MEN AND WOMEN

constitution, and men are more yang. Women are warmer inside than men, and this warmth is found in the quality of the eggs in the ovaries. Men on the other hand are cooler inside; the quality of sperm is also cool. A central aim of Taoist practice is to balance the yin/yang, female/male, and earth/heaven forces.

THE PALACES AND CONSTELLATIONS

As we have previously noted, the star world is divided into five parts called the *five palaces*, which are the five regions of the celestial sphere defined by projecting the four directions and the center into the heavens. In Chinese astrology, the five palaces and the twenty-eight lunar mansions (periods of the lunar zodiac) are fundamental. The twenty-eight constellations are divided into four groups of seven around the central palace. There are 182 stars in these twenty-eight constellations. In the past the four groups of constellations were believed to comprise four giant constellations. These mythical animals were called the guardians of the four palaces.

Eastern Palace—Green Dragon (32 Stars)
Northern Palace—Blue Turtle (35 Stars)
Western Palace—White Tiger (51 Stars)
Southern Palace—Red Bird (64 Stars)

In the advanced Taoist immortality practices of *Kan* and *Li*, the palaces are connected with the hands and feet. Through the connection of the

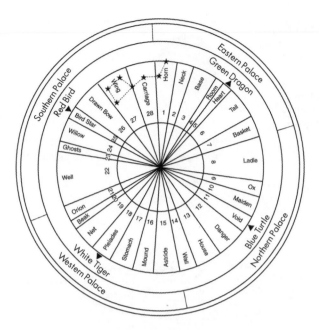

STAR PALACES AND CONSTELLATIONS

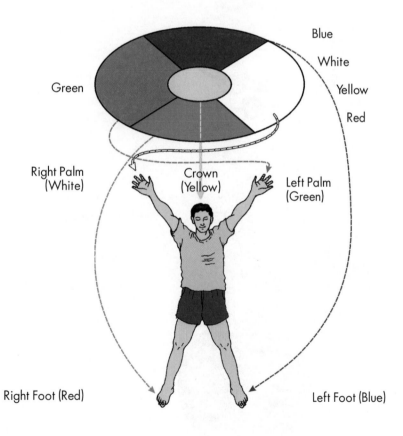

FIVE PALACES AND COLORS

Long ago the planets were seen as special stars related to the five elements:

Fire Star = Mars
Earth Star = Saturn
Metal Star = Mercury
Wood Star = Jupiter

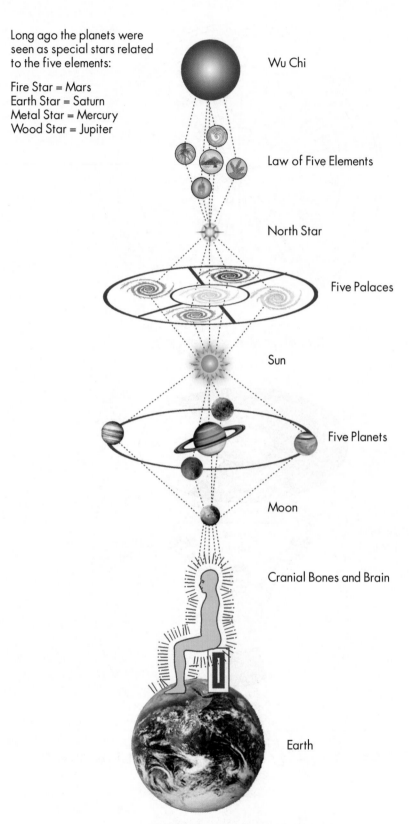

Wu Chi

Law of Five Elements

North Star

Five Palaces

Sun

Five Planets

Moon

Cranial Bones and Brain

Earth

The Craniosacral System, Elements, Star Palaces, and Planetary Forces

UNIVERSAL FORCES

extremities and the crown with the five palaces we can integrate the galactic energy more easily.

The North Star is the balancing point above the five palaces, and the sun is the balancing point above the planets. The sun and the North Star are gates to a higher dimension and to higher energy frequencies in the universe. The earth and moon are used to keep the grounding and to integrate high frequency energies in the physical body. In order to pass through sun and North Star gates, balance and integration of the underlying energies are required.

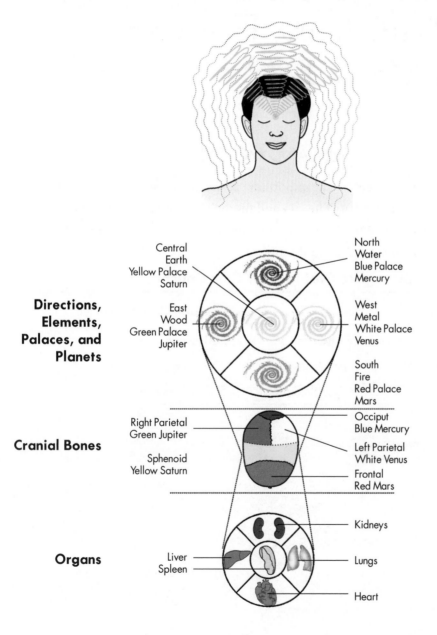

Directions, Elements, Palaces, and Planets

Central
Earth
Yellow Palace
Saturn

North
Water
Blue Palace
Mercury

East
Wood
Green Palace
Jupiter

West
Metal
White Palace
Venus

South
Fire
Red Palace
Mars

Cranial Bones

Right Parietal
Green Jupiter

Sphenoid
Yellow Saturn

Occiput
Blue Mercury

Left Parietal
White Venus

Frontal
Red Mars

Organs

Liver
Spleen

Kidneys

Lungs

Heart

INTEGRATING THE DIFFERENT FREQUENCIES IN THE CRANIUM

How to Use Planetary Forces in Your Life

SUN AND MOON

The sun/moon balance is an important preparatory practice. (See also Meditation 1 in chapter 10). The sun and moon energies were a major influence in the development of human consciousness as it evolved from more primitive life forms (mammals and reptiles).

Biological Evolution of Consciousness

Area of Brain	Approximate Time Formed
Neocortex: Self-Consciousness, Human	200 million years ago
Limbic System: Feelings, Emotions, Mammal State	300 million years ago
Brain Stem: Basic Life Features, Reptile State	500 million years ago

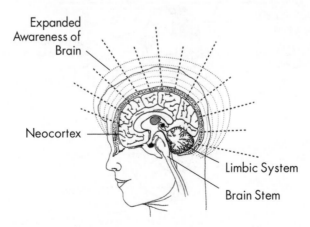

Expanded Awareness of Brain

Neocortex

Limbic System

Brain Stem

LIMBIC SYSTEM, BRAIN STEM, AND NEOCORTEX

The development of the neocortex as well as the etheric brain is the product of 500 million years of evolution. About 100 million years ago, the multiple-layer structure of the neocortex was formed. This process is still evolving. At the highest level of awareness, the neocortex expands energetically beyond the physical boundaries of the skull. This expanded "aural brain" connects one to the higher, godly levels, and facilitates clairvoyant vision and enlightenment. These auras have been depicted as golden crowns or halos in paintings of Christian saints.

The hot essence of accumulated yang energy generates fire and gives birth to the sun. The cold essence of accumulated yin energy makes water and gives birth to the moon. The sun's "cloud soul" and moon's "white soul" are the yang and yin manifestations of the energy around our planet.

The yang energy is manifested in three: heaven, sun, and constellations. The animal associated with sun energy is the three-legged crow. The sun crow stands for lively consciousness. Names that were used for the sun include "radiant numen" *(yao ling)* and "vermilion luminosity" *(chu ming)*.

As did most cultures, the Taoists saw the sun as the supreme, life-giving force on earth. It is the grand yang energy. The sun crow belongs to the west and has a metal energy. It is of the "yin class" and in this way clarifies and balances the light of the sun.

The moon is the grand yin energy, and is complementary to the sun. The moon animal is the toad; its nature is cold and watery. The moon toad belongs to the east and has a wood energy. It is of the "yang class," thus strengthening and illuminating the moon. Notice that the animals that correspond to the sun and moon have important counterbalancing qualities; one always finds a balancing element in Taoist medicine.

The moon plays a vital role, and its value is frequently underestimated. The moon is associated with female energy, and the lack of appreciation of the role of the moon is related to the low social status of women in the East and the unbalanced view of male/female energy around the world. The moon represents "potential"; it is the receptive form of spirit. Its true brightness is latent and dependent on the light of the sun, but its cool yin energy is constant and independent.

The moon is the magic mirror, reflecting the consciousness and light of the sun and bringing them to the core of the body, to our sexual potential. The water energy of the moon is closely related to the sexual energy and all body fluids. The phases of the moon strongly influence all fluids in the body and therefore human behavior. The moon energy finds its most important entrance point to the body in the sacrum. It represents the unconscious relation to the past, sexuality, and basic instinctive reactions. The moon's journey around the earth represents the yin principle in the cosmos and in our world.

The sun has a connection with the third eye and the pituitary gland. It is the star connected with consciousness and future vision. It functions as a source of consciousness and compassion and as a gate to the higher universe. The sun is also connected to the heart center, and has a controlling and regulating effect on the heart energy.

The sun and moon energies contribute to keeping a balance between the lower Tan Tien (belly) and the middle Tan Tien (heart). Imbalances can also relate to the influences from the planets. When the five planets are not in balance, it is hard to receive the deep frequencies of the sun, and the sexual energy becomes distorted. A strong connection to the sun will have a balancing function throughout the whole body.

Once the sun energy is collected in the heart, and the moon energy is collected in the sexual center, these two energies can be moved toward the lower Tan Tien. The most vital blood channels in the body, the aorta and the vena cava, can be used for this. The artery system, which the aorta belongs to, distributes the blood outward. It works with clear, red, oxygenated blood. It is a more yang/future-oriented system, so it has more sun qualities. The vein structure, including the vena cava, withdraws the blood from the outside. Dark or bluish blood is transported here, which will first go through the kidneys to be purified. It is a more yin/past-oriented system and has more moon qualities. Harmonizing the aorta and vena cava and the rest of the cardiovascular system will magnify the sun and moon meditations.

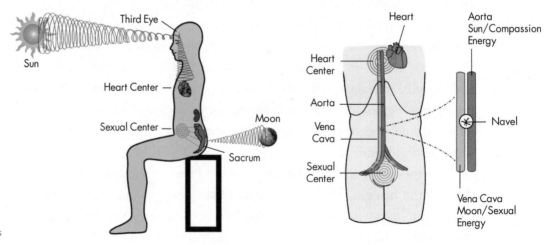

SUN AND MOON ENERGY CHANNELS IN THE BODY

A strong moon connection can give access to deeper, unconscious behavior and enable us to shine a light in the dark or transform unconsciousness into consciousness. The sexual essence, governed by the moon energy, will stimulate all energies in the body, both positive and negative. A strong stimulus of moon energy without an open sun connection can cause emotional problems and distorted sexual behavior.

In the Taoist way of energy cultivation, the sun controls the hours between midnight and noon (yang energy). The moon controls the hours between noon and midnight (yin energy). Sometimes it is said that all hours of sleep before midnight count double because of the strong yin energy that charges us at that time.

Taoist masters also saw the sun and moon as the eyes of heaven, corresponding to human eyes. The left eye, which is connected to the rational or intellectual part of the brain, relates to the sun, while the right eye, which is connected to the more intuitive part of the brain, relates to the moon.

Moon

Sun

MOON AND SUN EYES

We can use the sun and moon energies to create balance between the two hemispheres of the brain. Always integrate the sun and moon energies in the heart center, third eye, and the sexual center/sacrum before using the sun and moon energies during meditation. This is to prevent overheating the heart. In volume one of *Taoist Cosmic Healing*, we learned to create a Chi field and to call forth the energies of the elements for use in healing. This simple meditation is another example of how to utilize the elements. Using the power of the mind, bring the yang sun Chi *and* the yin moon Chi into the heart center, the third eye, and the sexual center. Imagine the golden sun Chi blending with the silver moon Chi in each center. See the two colors spiral together into clean, light, balanced pearls of white light inside the body. Once the pearls of balanced Chi have been established, stop and rest and allow this energy to flow into the rest of the body.

It is important to utilize the moon and sun frequencies to get a balance between water and fire energy in the body and then to increase the levels of both energies. The moon's color is yellow, its essence is red, and its rays are silver-white. The Taoist practices for the moon are done according to the eight articulations of the moon power, which occur during the two solstices, the two equinoxes, and the first day of the four seasons.

The following diagram, from a second-century Taoist text, shows the interaction of the sun and moon in relation to the twelve directions and the five elements.

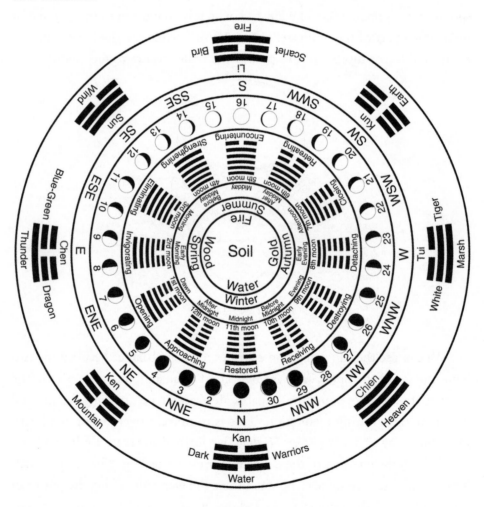

METHOD OF THE ELIXIR

MARS AND MERCURY

Mars and Mercury are the planets of fire and water, respectively. They are on a lower vibration level than the sun.

Mars is the planet of fire. Mars relates to the tongue, speech, and the physical heart. Mars energy is more male and future oriented. If the Mars energy is too strong in relation to the other energies, one may get aggressive and too talkative. This is often caused by weakness of the kidneys. Most heart problems are caused by depletion of the kidneys and the sexual energy. If Mars is too weak, the heart function/fire is withdrawn and the person feels weak.

The kidneys are the seat of the sexual essence and store the ancestral energy; they have a governing function on the sexual center. If the kidneys are depleted, sexual energy will also be weak. Fire is inactive in isolation and needs the presence of the other elements to stay balanced.

The play between water and fire is found in the controlling cycle of the five elements. Mars and the sun can be seen as fire qualities; Mercury and the moon are water qualities. This demonstrates the double nature in the fire element (primary and secondary fires) and the double formation of the water element (urogenital system).

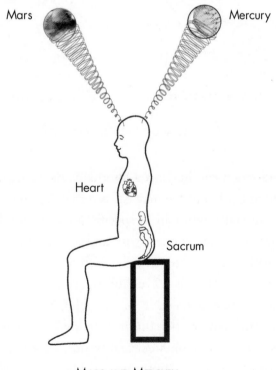

MARS AND MERCURY

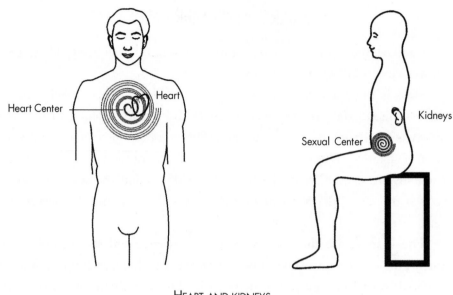

HEART AND KIDNEYS

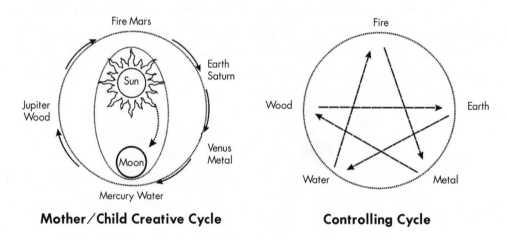

Mother/Child Creative Cycle   **Controlling Cycle**

CREATIVE AND CONTROLLING CYCLES

The sun and moon can be placed internally. As we mentioned earlier in this chapter and in book one, we may use external energies internally, so one may place the sun and moon Chi in specific places in the body for specific reasons. Similarly, one may connect with and use all of the elements. In the five-element creative cycle, water will give birth to wood, wood to fire, fire to earth, and earth to metal. It is a cycle of expansion and contraction in five stages (see *Fusion of the Five Elements* by Mantak Chia).

In the Taoist spiritual practice this interaction is compared with cooking. Water controls fire. If the kidneys/sexual (water) energy potential dries up, one cannot control the heart (fire) energy. The water energy of the kidneys/sexual center has a cooling and balancing effect on the fire energy of the heart center. On the other hand, if the fire is too weak, the body can get very cold and the spine and hip area can become very stiff. At the same time there is a controlling cycle that balances the five elements. The controlling cycle relates to elements that "control" other elements. For example, water controls fire by being able to drench it and put it out.

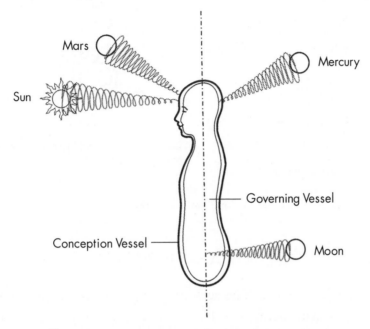

CONCEPTION AND GOVERNING VESSELS INTERACT WITH PLANETS
The conception vessel connects to Mars and the sun, the governing vessel connects to Mercury and the moon.

The sun/moon meditation and to a lesser degree the Mars/Mercury meditation can help people who have problems integrating their experiences of the past and balancing their concerns for the future. Today many people are stuck in past experiences. These experiences have an emotional charge and are related to pain that may be constantly denied or intellectually repressed. For these people, the sun connection will bring relief, more vision of the future, and another view of their past. Others strive only for future experiences and run away from themselves constantly. The moon/Mercury meditations will bring them closer to where they come from and to the forces and influences that have shaped their emotional body.

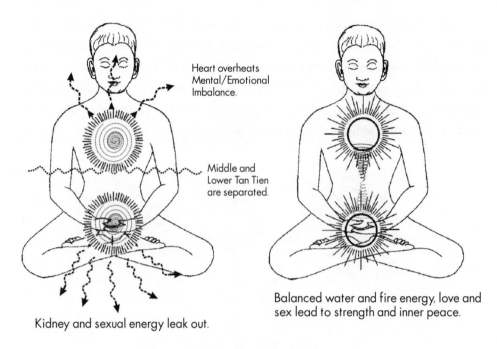

Heart overheats
Mental/Emotional
Imbalance.

Middle and
Lower Tan Tien
are separated.

Kidney and sexual energy leak out.

Balanced water and fire energy, love and
sex lead to strength and inner peace.

BALANCING WATER AND FIRE

VENUS AND JUPITER

The distinction between left-brain activity and right-brain activity has been a popular topic for many decades. Studies have shown that the left brain governs thinking that is more sequential, analytical, objective, and that tends to focus on parts. The right brain governs thinking that is more random, intuitive, subjective, and that tends to focus on wholes. Our focus points in heaven and the body determine how we perceive this reality.

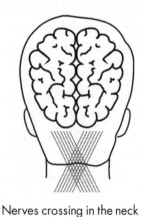

Nerves crossing in the neck

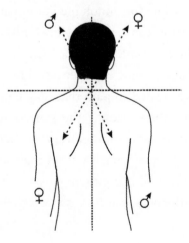

DISTINCT LEFT AND RIGHT BRAIN FUNCTIONS

The wood element force has a strong influence on the right side of the body, the metal element force on the right, and the earth element force in the middle, which acts as a balance. This is a direct influence from the realm of spiritual law straight down to the physical body. The central stabilizing earth aspect is also found in the energy of the spleen and pancreas.

The white stars and Venus activate the left, more rational part of the brain, which is traditionally associated with male energy. The green stars and Jupiter activate the right, more emotional part of the brain, which is traditionally associated with female energy.

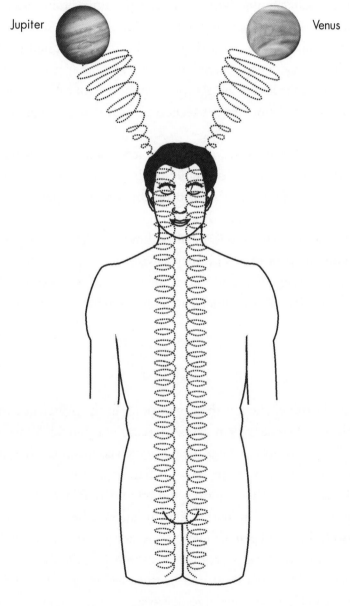

JUPITER AND VENUS

The nerves cross in the neck, so the left brain regulates the right side of the body, with the liver as the center point. The right brain regulates the left side of the body, with the spleen and the pancreas as the center point. These energies then enter more directly into the organs and body system.

The right brain is related to individual body and emotional awareness, and has a downward energy related to the spleen. The left brain deals mostly with social, external, and rational activities, and has a rising energy related to the liver and gall bladder.

The neocortex (the most complex part of the human brain) developed from the mammalian limbic system. In more primitive brain states, the mental and social abilities are very limited. The limbic system has a basic center in both hemispheres of the brain. This center, called the amigdala, deals with deep emotional experiences (affection, safety, and other primal needs). The human neocortex facilitates the ability to connect with other people and the universe. But we must not forget to be in touch with our feelings and our body.

If the right brain is overactive and the left-brain energy is blocked, the person tends to feel isolated, overemotional, and stuck in the past (with no spirit connection). If the left brain is overactive and the right-brain energy is blocked, the person has a hard time getting in touch with the emotions and body awareness. They tend to rationalize things and have a hard time feeling involved with others or even with themselves.

A left/right brain balance is crucial for a state of well-being. The planetary and star meditations can be a tremendous help in keeping or creating this balance.

SATURN

The universal earth element is the center point in the planetary and star system. It balances the energies of Mars/Mercury and Jupiter/Venus. It is also related with the central thrusting channel, which connects the crown with the perineum. The elemental earth force of Saturn meets the elemental earth force of the earth in the solar plexus and middle Tan Tien. The Saturn and earth quality is of major importance in balancing the energy in the solar plexus between liver and gall bladder on one side and the spleen and stomach on the other. Bodily stress is created by an imbalance between the internal and external world, primarily stored in the solar plexus. These days many people have trouble with their digestive system. Men tend to get a blocked and overheated liver and gall bladder, caused by irritation and anger. Women often suffer from spleen weakness, caused by worry and doubt, from which kidney imbalances originate. Saturn energy has a strong balancing effect that is often experienced physically in the skull during meditations, in the form of movements, pain, or pressure.

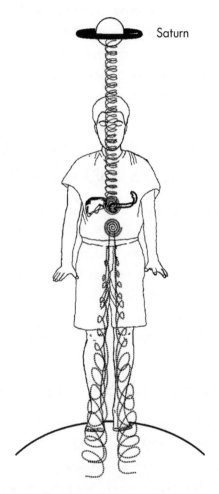

LET THE SATURN FORCE GO DOWN THROUGH THE PERINEUM.

HOW TO FIND YOUR STRONGEST AND WEAKEST PLANETS OF INFLUENCE

The easiest way discover which planet is your planet of strongest and weakest influence is to observe how you connect with the qualities, colors, and pictures that are associated with each planet. Observe the reactions in your body, and feel the energy that arises. If you take some time focusing on each planet, you will soon find which quality/element feels the most natural and easy to you. At the same time, you will also feel what is missing. If you study the typical qualities of each planet, you will recognize much in your daily life. (Also, use the meditations in chapter 10.) Regular evaluation will soon reveal that the energy of one of the planets is always present and that the energy of another may be deficient. It is interesting to meet people who have an abundance of the qualities we are missing. These individuals have something to teach us, but we may not like them because we may feel that they confront us too much. Observe and feel where and how they get this energy. Remember that the first goal is the sun state—the state of compassion that grows out of the virtues of all the organs and planets.

BREAKING THROUGH THE CIRCLE OF ATTRACTIONS AND ADDICTIONS

Balancing the planetary, galactic, and elemental forces helps us to clearly see the underlying causes of many problems in life, such as emotional patterns, addictions, irresponsible behaviors, and low self-esteem. At an emotional level, these patterns can only be temporarily released; at a mental level, they are often ignored or rigidly controlled. When we see the higher meaning and origin of these problems, and correct the information and energy imbalances that are causing them, they lose their reason for existing and gradually dissolve.

THE THREE TRANS-SATURNAL PLANETS

The three trans-Saturnal planets are not commonly used in the Eastern astrological systems because they were undiscovered until the last century. They can be seen as the higher octaves or frequencies of the nearer planets, which reflect the coevolution of human consciousness with universal changes.

Water	Mercury	Uranus	Thyroid Gland
Metal	Venus	Neptune	Thymus Gland
Fire	Mars	Pluto	Adrenal Gland

It is not necessary to work with these planets in your meditations, but they can be used to provide an extra dimension. Sometimes they come up spontaneously during meditation. Because of their influence on the social field, they often arise in group meditations.

In the Universal Tao System, eight planets are used with the eight energies of the *pa kua*, as seen in the illustration on page 133.

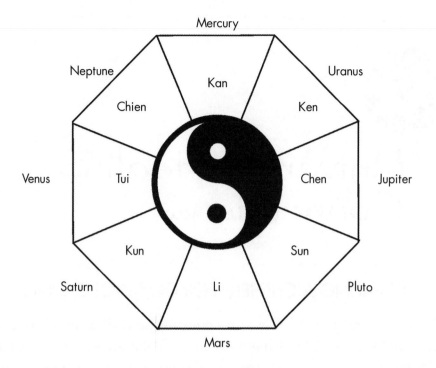

PA KUA AND PLANETS

More study and meditation will bring clearer information on Uranus, Neptune, and Pluto, as well as their cranial connection. The trans-Saturnal planets are the field between the basic planets (which correspond to the organs) and the stars (which correspond to the glands). They work on the lower frequency and the more physical, hormonal function of the glands.

According to our experiences and those of other practitioners during group meditations, the following entrance points can be used for the trans-Saturnal planets.

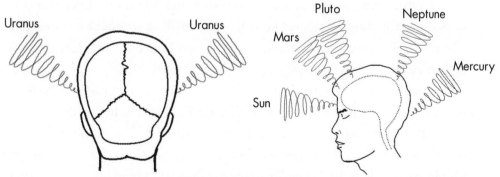

ENTRANCE POINTS FOR THE TRANS-SATURNAL ENERGIES
Pluto enters above the Mars area, Neptune around the hair spiral area above the Mercury area, and Uranus at an angle of about 45°, just a few centimeters above the ears.

9

Universal Healing Connections

CREATING A CHI FIELD FOR COSMIC HEALING

Up to this point in this book, we have primarily provided a conceptual foundation and framework for Taoist cosmology and the advanced Universal Tao healing practices. We will now turn our attention to some of the most important Universal Tao practices.

Fundamental to working with Chi is creating a Chi field, which is a containment area for all the Chi you might want for your Chi practice. The area can be as large or as small as you want. It can cover a city, a farm, your neighborhood, your home, a room, a group of people, or just yourself. You can create Chi fields within Chi fields, as many as you like.

Use your power of visualization to project a dome-shaped, protective covering around yourself, a group of people, or whatever suits your situation. Think of the dome as a semipermeable membrane that will allow Chi in but will not allow it to leak out. It will also prevent unwanted forces or emanations from coming into your space, somewhat like the ozone layer that protects the earth. The dome may be as large or small as you want it to be. This Chi field will contain the universal, cosmic, and environmental Chi that you draw into it.

You can create a Chi field to protect your house. In rural areas, Chi fields have been used to protect and fortify farmlands, resulting in greatly enriched produce and increased yields of agricultural products. We should also cover ourselves with a Chi field when we do our Chi cultivation practices. Teachers should create a Chi field in order to impart more powerful experiences when guiding students in meditative processes. Cosmic Healing practitioners should create a Chi field for a powerful healing environment.

To prepare a Chi field for use in healing, first connect with the forces of the six directions (north, south, east, west, above, and below) and create a Chi field. Creating a Chi field is very important. Sense the power of thunder and lightning filling the Chi field with energy. Create a domed Chi field to cover the room you are doing a healing session in. Sense that the room has become electrified. Draw in the power of the lakes, forests, oceans, sun, stars, and high mountains. When you are ready, inhale and draw in the energy from the galaxy and universe.

Next, be aware of your lower Tan Tien, and draw up this energy and pour it over the crown. Feel the energy come to your crown and let the energy flow. Feel numbness and tingling. Focus on the soles of the feet.

Gradually feel that the room has become charged with universal Chi. Imagine a bright star about six inches above your head. This is your personal star, and it can be used like a computer to customize Chi from outside sources for your personal use. It can also be used to connect yourself to others or bring energy from outside sources directly into the crown point. Close your eyes and feel the personal stars of all the individuals participating in the healing session. Visualize all the personal stars becoming linked by a line of energy, beginning in the left corner of the room and continuing in a clockwise direction. Visualize the line of energy spiraling out clockwise to link all the participants' personal stars with your own personal star. Next, project an energy body above you in the dome. (See *Taoist Cosmic Healing* for detailed instruction about projecting an energy body.) Then project an individual vertical connection from the energy body to each participant. Link all the stars, including your own star, to the energy body.

The size and shape of the energy body is not important; just have the idea and the sense that it is there for you to use. This tool provides you with an immediate resource to draw from when you distribute energy to the participants. When you are guiding and teaching a meditative process, keep your awareness of your lower Tan Tien and the universe, and guide the students via the energy body for enhanced power and effectiveness. You may do this by telling the students to imagine the Chi in the energy body doing specific things and then telling them to visualize that Chi streaming down from the energy body and going into or through the physical body of each person in the room.

For yourself, relax the analytic mind and let it sink down into the lower Tan Tien. Fill the lower Tan Tien with Smiling Sunshine Chi. (See *Taoist Cosmic Healing* for instruction in this practice.) Be aware of your heart; let love, joy, and happiness fill the lower Tan Tien. Extend the Chi in your lower Tan Tien up to the universe, multiply its energy, draw it down to the energy body, and then distribute this energy to those present.

ACTIVATING THE THREE FIRES AND HEALING WITH THE CHI FIELD

The Universal Tao practices strengthen our connection to the universe and open us up to the primordial force of the cosmos and the energy within nature. We are dynamically connected to the infinite. "As above, so below" is an echo of wisdom heard from sages and mystics throughout the ages. When we can connect to and absorb the energy that surrounds us, we are able to tap into the many splendors of the universe.

We exist because of the unique combination of the forces that are around and within us. The two main forces are electricity and magnetism. *Bioelectromagnetism* is the Western term for life force and what the Tao refers to as Chi. For the last five thousand years, the Taoists have utilized bioelectromagnetism to enhance their way of life and to establish a relationship with the universe. *Bio* signifies life, *electro* refers to the universal (yang) energies of the stars and planets, and *magnetism* refers to the (yin) earth force or gravitational force present on all planets and stars. As we align ourselves with these forces, we become a conduit through which we can absorb and digest these energies through the body, mind, and spirit, thus establishing a direct connection with the universe. The Taoists recognized this connection and created the Chi Kung practices to enhance our relationship to and our understanding of this connection.

Humans normally access bioelectromagnetic energy through food and air. Plants take the universal energies of the sun and the magnetic energies of the earth and digest and transform them, thereby making these energies available to all living beings. Taoists believe that the food sources with the purest form of energy are the green leafy vegetables, which have taken sunlight directly into their cells. Rather than waiting until the energy in the universe is processed through plants, the Taoist goes directly to the source of this primordial energy. There are various meditational Chi Kung exercises that enable practitioners to directly tap into the energy of the universe and direct this energy precisely.

An important Universal Tao practice is the activation of the *three fires*, which are the three sources of fire energy contained within the lower abdomen (the lower Tan Tien), the "door of life" (the adrenal/kidney fire at the Ming Men point), and the heart center. Opening these centers fills the body with energy and life force.

1. Stand with the feet together. Feel the connection to the earth through the soles of the feet. Project your mind and extend your Chi into the earth. Continue extending your mind power and Chi until you feel the connection to the infinite space beyond the earth.

2. Hold the palms down, parallel to the ground, lifting up the fingers. Connect to the earth energy through the center of the palms.

3. Move the arms and palms out slightly to the front of the body (palms still facing down). As the arms move, expand your mind and feel the connection to the earth and the infinite space below you.

4. Gently pull the hands and arms back toward the body. As the arms move, feel the Chi flowing through your body and condensing into the lower Tan Tien. Continue to push and pull the energy with your arms and palms six to nine times, expanding your mind and gathering Chi from the infinite space into the lower Tan Tien.

5. Lift your arms and face the palms toward the lower Tan Tien. Feel as if you are holding a huge Chi ball on the lower Tan Tien. Feel the connection between the fire in the lower Tan Tien and the fire energy in the universe. Feel the warmth spread through the entire body.

6. Expand your awareness to the infinite space behind you. Move your hands to the back and hold a huge Chi fire ball on the door of life (the adrenal/kidney or Ming Men area, which is located between the second and third lumbar vertebrae just beneath the two kidneys and opposite the navel).

7. Feel the Chi ball pulsing and breathing, drawing energy into the body from the infinite space behind you.

8. Lift the hands, palms facing up, to the sides of the body under the arm pits. Feel the Chi from the fingers extend into your chest igniting the fire in the heart center.

9. Allow the heart center to open, pulsing and breathing with Chi.

10. Feel all three fires (the lower Tan Tien, the door of life, and the heart center) activated and resonating together.

To further activate the fire of the lower Tan Tien, feel the energy behind and below the navel become warm as you direct a golden sunshine smile down from your face. Imagine that the energy in your abdomen is like a fireball. Create a stove burning with fire close to the sacrum and lower lumbar vertebrae. It is helpful to use the breath and to imagine the breath fanning the fire. The Taoists describe it as a burning stove that energizes the other fires in the body.

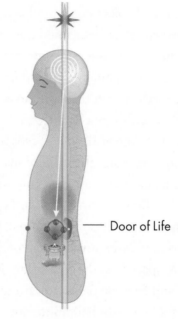

Smile down to the abdomen to create a burning stove near the lower lumbar and sacrum. Create a fireball behind the navel above the stove.

—— Door of Life

LOWER TAN TIEN FIRE

To further activate the fire of the door of life (the adrenal-kidney/Ming Men fire), be aware of the yang energy of the adrenals, which are above the kidneys. Move that yang energy down into the center of each kidney. This creates a "yang within yin" force, also known as the "fire under the sea." Expand the activated adrenal-kidneys energy to the Ming Men point on the spine opposite the navel and just below the kidneys.

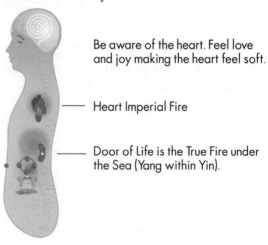

Be aware of the heart. Feel love and joy making the heart feel soft.

Heart Imperial Fire

Door of Life is the True Fire under the Sea (Yang within Yin).

MING MEN AND HEART FIRE

To further activate the fire of the heart center (also known as the *imperial fire*), smile down into the heart. Feel the fire of love, joy, happiness, and compassion creating softness in the heart. This will activate the consciousness of the heart. Then make a triangle, connecting the heart center with the Ming Men center and the lower Tan Tien. This triangulation doubles or triples the Chi fire power of the three fires.

TRIANGULATION OF THE THREE FIRES
Move from the Tan Tien up to the heart.

Another foundational Universal Tao practice involves activating the Chi field and energy body for use in healing.

1. Ask the participants to relax the analytic mind and sink their awareness down into the lower Tan Tien.
2. Connect with the energy body. Move your hands down. Touch your navel. Concentrate on the lower Tan Tien. Ask the participants to follow along with you. Your fingers touch the navel, then focus on the door of life. Feel a numbness, a tingling sensation of energy flow. When you feel it, transfer it up to the crown. Visualize the energy expanding into the universe, and multiply the feeling. Then guide and transfer the universal energy down to the energy body. Always spiral the energy in the lower Tan Tien. Imagine the lower Tan Tien in the energy body and see the energy spiral. Bring this energy down through the crown point and into the lower Tan Tien of your physical body. Use your mind to imagine a spiral of Chi that builds in strength in the lower Tan Tien. Feel your Chi condense as it clears any blockages in the abdominal area.

3. Take time to work with the lower Tan Tien. Transfer your Chi to the others present. When your lower Tan Tien is very full, you actually feel the energy charge up the whole brain. At this point, your brain has a lot of Chi to extend up to the universe.

4. At this level, there is no particular color for the energy body; it depends on what you are doing. Just transfer the Chi up through your body, through the energy body, and into the universe. When it multiplies, it will be abundant when it comes back down.

You cannot teach something that you do not first have yourself. When you are teaching, you are controlling the energy. You are guiding the students' energy, and helping them to understand and experience what you are teaching. If you are happy, they feel happy; if you feel joy, they feel joy. When you experience the feeling of the bone marrow, you transfer this to the students. The students can only be as sensitive and perceptive in working with the energy as you are at that moment. You may feel pain in your body at times. If you do, just pick out the good feeling and transfer that up, otherwise the students may feel pain that is not their own pain.

You have to multiply the energy that you are feeling first before transferring your energy to the students. Transfer what you are sensing (laughing bones, tingling, numbness, etc.) out to the universe. From there, spiral the energy a few times and multiply it, and then bring the increased Chi down to the energy body. It will then spread out to the participants by itself. (See illustration bottom of page 146.)

THE THREE MINDS

In the remainder of this chapter, we will explore several advanced Universal Tao practices. Before proceeding with these practices, it is important to be familiar with the Taoist principle of the "three minds" and able to combine the three minds into one.

Taoist masters discovered that human beings have three minds: the upper mind, which is the observing mind; the middle mind, which is the consciousness mind; and the lower mind, which is the awareness mind (see illustration opposite). The upper mind is valuable for analytic activity and planning, but negative emotions can cause the upper mind to be agitated with excessive thinking and worrying, which drains energy. The upper mind works practically all the time, stirring up the emotions and using up to 80 percent of our body energy. We should train the upper mind to be relaxed and to just observe when we do not need to be involved in specific mental activity. The key is to "seek the released mind" by relaxing, emptying, and sinking the upper mind down into the lower mind. Western science has recently discovered that there are nerve endings in the stomach and intestines that are related to emotional responses. By smiling into the lower Tan Tien, we can activate the lower mind. We can then use the upper mind (observing mind), middle mind (consciousness mind), and lower mind (awareness mind) together, grounded in the abdomen.

If we can use the lower mind more, the upper mind can rest and listen (observe) from the abdomen. The upper mind, or, as the Taoists refer to it, the "monkey mind," can, when agitated, suppress consciousness or awareness. Once the upper mind rests, we can be conscious and aware of much that we were never conscious or aware of before. We can be at ease, save energy, and build up strength for any tasks.

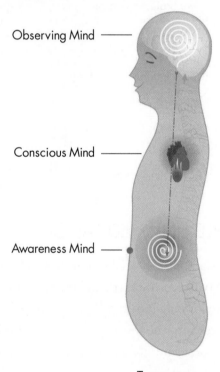

Observing Mind

Conscious Mind

Awareness Mind

THREE MINDS

Taoist masters fuse the three minds into one mind, known as Yi. To fuse the three minds, stand or sit, alone or with others, in meditation. Relax and empty the analytic mind. Let it sink into the lower Tan Tien by smiling down into your lower abdomen. Bring your awareness to your abdomen and fill your abdominal brain (lower mind) with Chi. When the abdomen is filled with Chi and feels nice and warm, it will rise and fill the upper brain/mind with Chi. Sink the upper mind and the middle mind into the lower Tan Tien, combining the three minds into one mind. The unified, three-mind power will move to the mid-eyebrow area. You can use this Yi to make correct decisions and to take the correct action or nonaction.

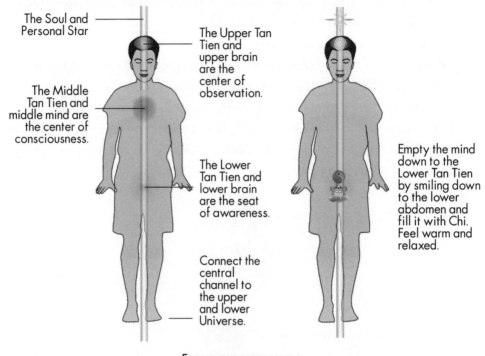

The Soul and Personal Star

The Upper Tan Tien and upper brain are the center of observation.

The Middle Tan Tien and middle mind are the center of consciousness.

The Lower Tan Tien and lower brain are the seat of awareness.

Connect the central channel to the upper and lower Universe.

Empty the mind down to the Lower Tan Tien by smiling down to the lower abdomen and fill it with Chi. Feel warm and relaxed.

FUSING THE THREE MINDS

THE WORLD LINK MEDITATION

The "world link meditation" is a powerful meditation in which practitioners become a communication link between the earth and the universe. To do this practice, first you fuse the three minds into the Yi, as described above. The next step is to bring the Yi power into the third eye and expand it into the six directions of the universe (into the infinite space to the north, south, east, west, above, and below).

At this point, use the Yi power to connect to your personal star six inches above your head. Expand your awareness to encompass your personal star, then expand your consciousness out to the whole universe. If in a group, spiral out and link with the personal stars of everyone in the group. Create an energy body, linking everyone together with each other and with the universe. Continue to expand the awareness from the abdomen. Next, link all the personal stars and the energy body with the universe.

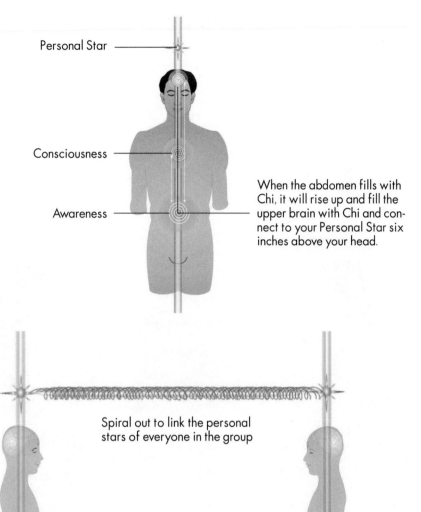

Personal Star

Consciousness

Awareness

When the abdomen fills with Chi, it will rise up and fill the upper brain with Chi and connect to your Personal Star six inches above your head.

Spiral out to link the personal stars of everyone in the group

LINK WITH THE OTHER PERSONAL STARS

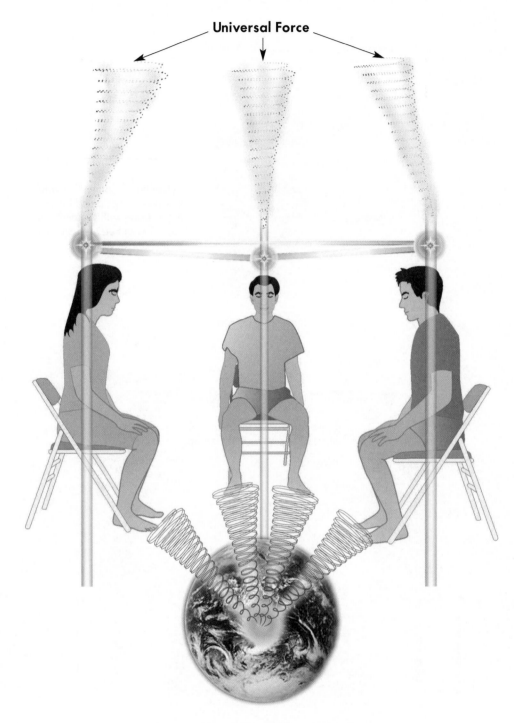

Universal Force

LINK PERSONAL STARS WITH UNIVERSAL FORCE

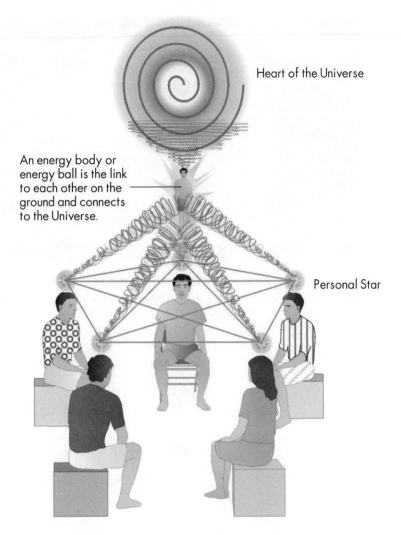

Heart of the Universe

An energy body or energy ball is the link to each other on the ground and connects to the Universe.

Personal Star

GROUP IS LINKED TO THE HEART OF THE UNIVERSE.

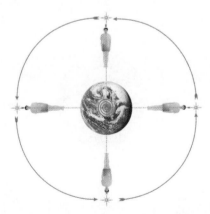

FORMING A COMMUNICATION LINK BETWEEN THE EARTH AND THE UNIVERSE
The world link meditators can connect with friends, other Universal Tao practitioners, or others who are doing similar work to form a communication network between the earth and the universe.

THE HEART OF THE UNIVERSE (GOD)
Linking to the heart of the universe, the world link meditators practice
"being in unconditional love."

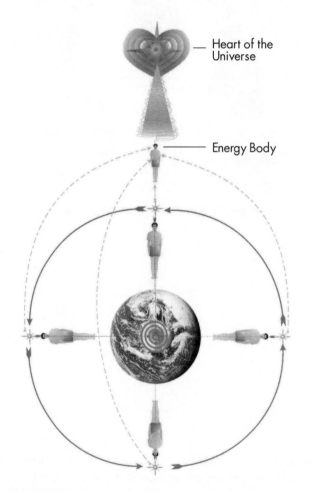

Heart of the Universe

Energy Body

WORLD LINK MEDITATION NETWORK, ENERGY BODY, AND HEART OF THE UNIVERSE

THE SACRED CIRCLE OF FIRE

The "sacred circle of fire" is a powerful practice that can protect us from all evil, whether it be sickness, misfortune, or the negative effects of the destructive thought patterns of those around us. It allows us to connect with the power of the universe. It also helps us remove doubts of our own worthiness so that we may reclaim the best that life has to offer, which is our birthright. The sacred circle of fire is a protective ring that connects us with the elemental essences and forces in the universe that both strengthen and protect us. To create the sacred circle of fire, we use a method of inner visualization that involves the power of the three minds (the observing mind, consciousness mind, and awareness mind) fused into one mind, the Yi. It enables us to get in touch with the guardian essence (guardian angel) and the forces of the six protective guardian animals of the six directions.

THE SACRED FIRE CIRCLE

First, activate the lower Tan Tien fire, the adrenal-kidney/Ming Men fire, and the heart center fire. Then fuse the three minds into one, and bring the Yi up to the third eye.

When we use awareness and consciousness, we turn our visualization into actualization. Using our trust and belief, we can manifest what we create in visualization with good intentions.

Next, visualize and imagine a big cauldron burning with fire in the cosmos (see page 148, bottom). Feel the awareness and let it happen.

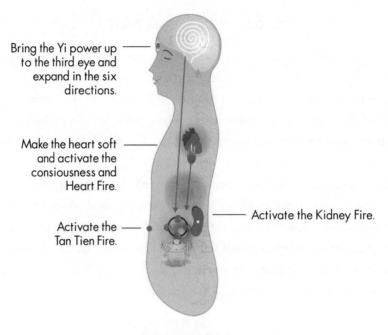

Bring the Yi power up to the third eye and expand in the six directions.

Make the heart soft and activate the consiousness and Heart Fire.

Activate the Tan Tien Fire.

Activate the Kidney Fire.

FIRES AND YI

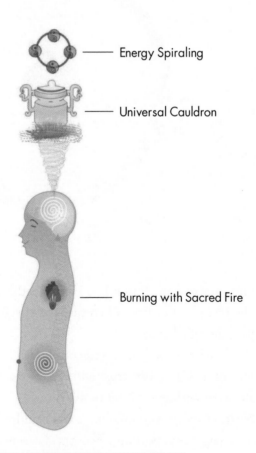

Energy Spiraling

Universal Cauldron

Burning with Sacred Fire

PROJECT A CAULDRON OF FIRE BURNING IN THE COSMOS

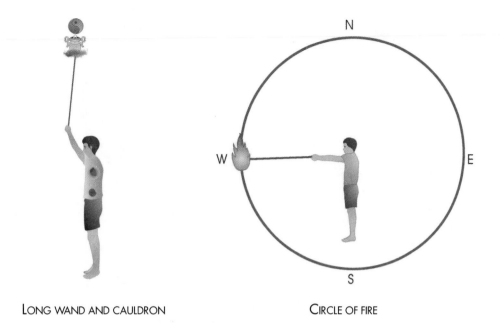

LONG WAND AND CAULDRON   CIRCLE OF FIRE

Now, visualize yourself holding a long wand. Reach out to the cauldron and ignite the wand with fire.

Then use the Yi power to draw on the ground with the burning wand a circle of fire that is seven feet (two meters) in diameter.

Stand in the center. Face the north. Imagine the burning wand, and light up the northern section outside the circle with fire. Pass the wand in an arc toward the south edge of the circle and ignite the southern section with fire. Then swing it to the eastern edge and ignite that section with fire. Next swing it to the western edge and ignite the western section with fire.

Now expand the fire to the whole circle. This circle of fire will protect you from all evil, whether it be in the form off sickness, misfortune, or negativity. Place the wand at the edge of the circle.

At this point, squat down facing north. In each direction place, through visualization, a protective animal (guardian essence or angel). In front of you (north) place a blue tortoise, in back (south) a red pheasant, to the right (east) a green dragon, to the left (west) a white tiger, above (center) a yellow phoenix, and below (earth) a black tortoise.

Next, create a protective golden dome Chi field over you. Let go of all concerns and empty yourself. Ask each animal for protection. These protective animals of the six directions are the same protective animals that are associated with the vital organs. For energetic protection, ask the blue tortoise for gentleness, the red pheasant for joy, the green dragon for kindness, the white tiger for courage, the yellow phoenix for fairness, and the black tortoise for

IGNITING THE FOUR DIRECTIONS

stillness. Connect with the force of universal love, saying "I am worthy of divine love and protection."

Remain in this position for several minutes. Be aware of the sacred fire burning all around the circle and the golden dome Chi field surrounding you. This forms a permanent, magnetic sacred circle that is literally indestructible.

GOLDEN DOME CHI FIELD

HEALING VISUALIZATIONS

There are a number of Universal Tao practices for affirming peace within your heart and healing yourself. We will explore several of these practices in the remainder of this chapter.

Begin with the following practice of affirmation. First, calm the mind, emptying the upper mind down into the abdomen and lower Tan Tien. Direct the consciousness of the heart down to the awareness of the lower Tan Tien. Combine the three minds to fuse into the one mind (Yi). Expand the Yi awareness out to the universe. The Yi mind is the most powerful mind to use when connecting with the universe.

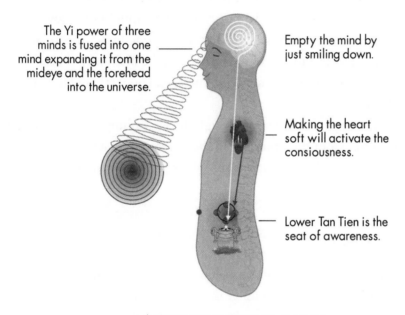

The Yi power of three minds is fused into one mind expanding it from the mideye and the forehead into the universe.

Empty the mind by just smiling down.

Making the heart soft will activate the consiousness.

Lower Tan Tien is the seat of awareness.

ACTIVATE THREE MINDS INTO ONE MIND

Now, repeat the following affirmations from the center of your awareness and consciousness, following the instructions associated with each statement.

I am at peace, feeling love and compassion in myself (touch your heart).
I am calm, warm, and still in my center (touch your lower abdomen).
I am at peace with my family and people close to me (picture them).
I am at peace with my neighbors (picture them).
I am at peace with my friends and coworkers (picture them).
I am at peace with my community (picture them).
I am at peace with myself and all sentient beings (feel them).

Personal Healing Visualization

Below is a simple but powerful personal healing visualization:

1. Empty the mind by starting a smile on your face. Let the smiling energy flow down to the neck and into the heart area (the seat of consciousness). Make the heart feel soft and full of love, joy, and happiness, activating the conscious mind.
2. Continue smiling and relaxing the mind down to the abdomen (the center of awareness). Smile, emptying the mind and senses (eyes, ears, nose, and mouth) down until the navel area feels warm, activating the awareness.
3. Feel the observing mind of the head and the conscious mind of the heart going down to combine with the awareness mind of the lower Tan Tien. Combine and fuse these three minds into one mind, the Yi, at the mid-eyebrow. Expand the awareness out from the abdomen beyond your physical body to the cosmos and universe, connecting with the universal energy.
4. Take the Yi and spiral it upward through the crown into the vast energy of the universe. Continue spiraling in the universe and let the energy in the Yi multiply. Then, spiral it down to your personal star and into your whole body.

Forest Green Energy

You can continue with this healing practice by picturing an ancient forest with bright green leaves reaching up in the universe. Then picture a beautiful, emerald green light coming from heaven, and spiral the green light down to you. Spiral the green light down through your community, your home, and then into your crown. Let it clean your whole body, binding and absorbing any negativity, burdens, worries, and sick energy, and draining it all out of your body. Let it flow down deep into the ground. Visualize digging a hole and burying the sick, negative energy in the ground. Let your heart be happy. Repeat this three to six times, thirty-six to eighty-one times for serious illnesses.

FOREST GREEN ENERGY
Keep the lower Tan Tien warm and expand the Yi mind to the universe.
Picture a beautiful, emerald green light in the universe.

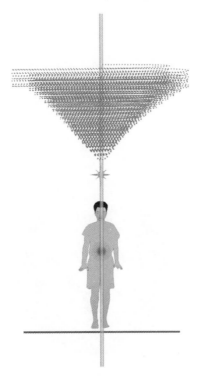

SPIRAL THE GREEN LIGHT DOWN
Spiral the healing light down through your community, your home,
and then into your crown.

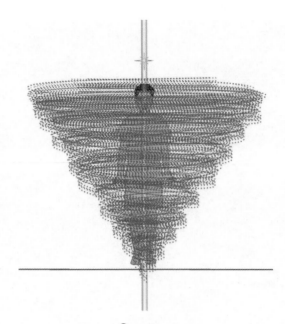

CLEANSING
Let the green, healing energy cleanse all that it comes into contact with.
Then spiral it down into the ground.

BURY THE SICK ENERGY
Picture digging a hole and burying the sick, negative energy deep into the ground,
never to return. It will be transformed by the earth into positive energy.

Universal Violet Energy

Continue your healing practice by picturing violet light, the most abundant energy in the universe. Imagine it coming from the North Star and the Big Dipper. Gather the energy in the cup of the Big Dipper. See yourself holding the handle of the Big Dipper and pouring the violet light down over your crown. Spiral the violet energy down, filling all the cells of your body, healing and strengthening the whole body. Repeat this six times.

THE NORTH STAR IS A MAJOR SOURCE OF VIOLET LIGHT

In the following variation of the violet light healing practice, you focus on the brain and specific organs:

1. Fill the brain with violet light, saying, "Let all sickness go away and let the brain be at its best."

2. Follow this method for each organ, using the same affirmation. You can also work with the organs in groups:
   Eyes, ears, nose, mouth, tongue, teeth;
   Thyroid, parathyroid, thymus, pancreas, prostate, uterus;
   Lungs, heart, stomach, small intestines, large intestines;
   Liver, spleen, kidneys, ovaries, testicles.

3. While practicing this visualization and series of affirmations, stay conscious of the lower Tan Tien. Expand your awareness to the universe and let the universe fill you with healing energy.

Activating the Immune System

The following practice activates and energizes the body's immune and defense systems:

1. Touch the sacrum and feel your fingers grow "long" with Chi and penetrate into the sacrum and bone marrow, activating the bone marrow.

2. Activate the lower Tan Tien. Expand your attention into the universe; connect with the universal energy. Allow the universal Chi to fill the sacrum and the whole body. Feel your whole body radiate, clean and shining with light.

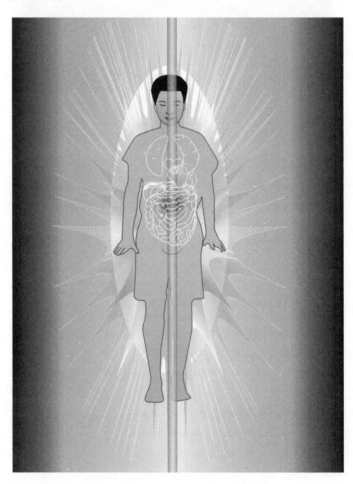

FEEL YOUR WHOLE BODY RADIATE LIGHT

3. Allow Chi to rise up the spine to the forehead. Feel pulsating in the temple bones. This increases the production of healthy white blood cells for the immune system.

ALLOW CHI TO RISE UP THE SPINE TO THE FOREHEAD

4. Keep the lower Tan Tien warm and feel the Chi flow up the spinal cord, then let it spiral up into the universe. The universe will fill you with healing energy.
5. Next, touch above the pubic bone and feel your fingers grow long with Chi, as before. Let them penetrate into the bone marrow to activate the immune system's production of red and white blood cells. Leave your fingers there and lower your mind into the lower Tan Tien. Feel the happy, laughing, and tingling sensations in the bones.

TOUCH THE PUBIC BONE, ACTIVATING THE IMMUNE SYSTEM

6. Touch the middle point of the femur bones (in the upper legs). Feel your fingers grow long with Chi, penetrating the bone marrow. This should give a tingling sensation through the whole leg. It also increases the production of red blood cells.

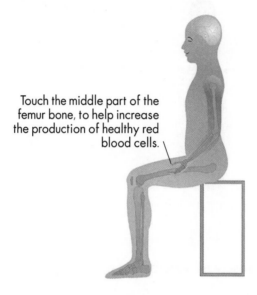

Touch the middle part of the femur bone, to help increase the production of healthy red blood cells.

TOUCH THE FEMUR BONES

7. Touch the middle point of the humerus bones (in the upper arms). Feel your fingers grow long with Chi, penetrating the bone marrow, activating production of healthy red blood cells.

8. Next, touch the sternum. Feel your fingers grow long with Chi, penetrating the bone marrow. Let the Chi spread throughout the sternum, then expand the Chi through the whole rib cage and chest cavity, activating the thymus gland.

9. Feel the connection to the thyroid and parathyroid glands, energizing them. This activates the immune system and increases the production of white blood cells and T-cells (T-cells are a type of white blood cell that protects you from viral infections, produces antibodies, and fights cancers).

Once a practitioner has an understanding of the various qualities of Chi and their effects, one may play with the energy and alter the practice to suit the needs of the moment. Strive to practice daily until Cosmic Healing Chi Kung becomes natural. Practice these guidelines and relax into who you are as a practitioner.

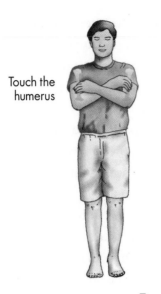

Touch the
humerus

Touch the
sternum

TOUCH THE HUMERUS AND STERNUM

TRANSFORMING NEGATIVE CONDITIONING
AND NEGATIVE THINKING

In order to maximize Chi and integrate it throughout the body, mind, and spirit, we need to get rid of subconscious guilt. Our subconscious guilt complexes are major obstacles to our health and progress, often causing illness and frustration. It is as if we have an inner program that tells us we do not deserve to have health, wealth, and happiness. We can never bring ourselves to ask the universe for anything that we do not feel worthy to receive. Humankind is naturally entitled to everything that the earth and the universe can provide for our happiness and well-being. As children of God we deserve the best.

Every thought, whether positive or negative, is a command to the universe. If our lives are not how we would like them to be, it is because we have unwittingly given negative commands to the cosmos. Humans have a deep need for love and attention, and sometimes we may try to get sympathy and attention through being sick, or by becoming a victim. Subconsciously, we may send out messages to the universe to make ourselves ill; the more attention that is given to sickness and ill health, the more energy that is received from the cosmos to make that happen. Therefore, we must be careful of what we think, feel, and say if we want our lives to change for the better.

We can remove all the unworthy, guilty, sinful thoughts and ideas, replacing them with the realization that we are the children of God or the cosmos.

We can accept the best the universe and earth have to offer. We need not accept the results of our negative thinking. We can initiate a positive course of action. To transform negative thinking and initiate a new direction, we must become conscious of negative thought patterns and replace them with new commands of the cosmic force.

To make a positive statement is to make a direct command. A command given in the present tense—in the now—is the most powerful command that we can give to the cosmos. A command to the cosmos should be phrased clearly, as an individual statement, and always said aloud.

For example, we can make the command: "I am well; I am healthy; I am happy; I am wealthy." It doesn't matter how sick or poor we are; the fact is, the moment we make this command, we have already begun to take on these qualities. The change begins very rapidly. The cosmic force begins to work on our inner functions immediately, according to what qualities we have claimed.

Success in using cosmic power depends upon how we work with and exercise our commands. Once we have set the cosmic force in motion with a direct command, we must take action. We must be willing to take responsibility for ourselves. The universe cannot accomplish everything on its own. The key is to use the cosmic force to aid our actions. If we work with the right intent, and are willing to take action and responsibility, there is no limit to what we can accomplish. Practicing Positive Mind Power, Fusing the Three Minds into One, and the Inner Smile will help.

Yi Mind Power Manifestation

The center of manifestation is the frontal lobe of the brain. We manifest our affirmations in the physical, emotional, mental, and spiritual body by visualizing our affirmation or cosmic command from the center of awareness and then broadcasting it out to the entire universe through the frontal lobe. The following Yi Mind Power practice cultivates and directs mind power to manifest the changes we desire in our lives.

1. Empty the mind by starting a smile on your face. Let the smiling energy flow down to the neck and into the heart area/seat of consciousness. Make the heart feel soft and full of love, joy, and happiness, activating the conscious mind.

2. Continue smiling and relaxing the mind down to the abdomen/center of awareness. Smile, emptying the mind and senses. Activate the center of awareness until the navel area feels warm.

3. Feel the observing mind of the head and the conscious mind of the heart going down to combine with the awareness mind of the lower Tan Tien. Combine and fuse these three minds into one mind, the Yi, at the mid-eyebrow.
4. Touch the sacrum, activating it and filling it with Chi.
5. Then move the Chi up to open the frontal lobe of the brain at the third eye/mid-eyebrow. Create a triangle from the third eye to the temple bones, filling it with Chi.

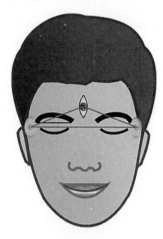

THIRD EYE AND TEMPLE BONES FORM A TRIANGLE

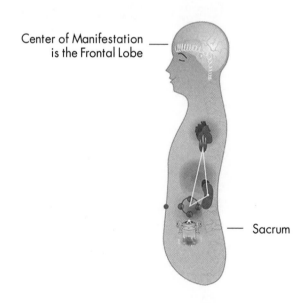

Center of Manifestation
is the Frontal Lobe

Sacrum

MANIFEST THE MIND POWER
Activate the frontal lobe by moving Chi up from the sacrum.

6. Place the attention in the abdomen. Visualize the thought that you want to manifest here. Then bring it up to the heart connection, then to the upper mind, the frontal lobe, and the mid-eyebrow. Now, broadcast it out to the entire universe. This affirmation is multiplied many times by the abundant universal energy. It will return to you to be manifested.

You can also use this practice to work with and heal your physical body, emotional body, and mental body. To work with your physical body and body image, first follow the steps outlined above, fusing the three minds into one (the Yi) at the mid-eyebrow, activating the sacrum, and filling the frontal lobe with Chi. Then picture yourself at an age you would like to be, and hold that image very clearly. Hold it in the lower abdomen and then move it up to the heart area. Continue to hold this image very clearly while moving it up to the upper mind, the frontal lobe, and the mid-eyebrow. Then send it out to the universe in all six directions, saying, "I am well and perfectly healthy."

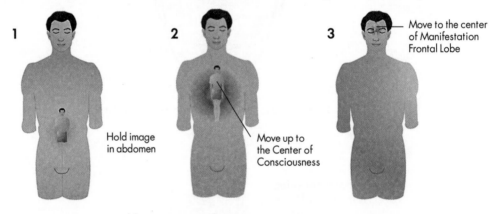

1

Hold image
in abdomen

2

Move up to
the Center of
Consciousness

3

Move to the center
of Manifestation
Frontal Lobe

MOVE THE IMAGE UP TO THE THIRD EYE

SEND THE IMAGE OUT INTO THE UNIVERSE

To work with your emotional body and emotional image, follow the initial steps above, and then visualize your emotional body: See a body-shaped image composed of all kinds of moving colors. Say to yourself: "I let go of old emotional experiences, seeing them for what they are. I fill myself with radiant joy, love, and compassion." Bring this image up to the heart center and then to the frontal lobe. Then send it out to the universe. The universe will multiply it many times and it will be sent back to you.

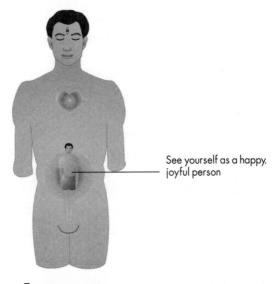

See yourself as a happy, joyful person

EMOTIONAL IMAGE

To work with your mental body and mental image, follow the initial steps above, and then visualize your mental body. See a body-shaped image composed of light, and say to yourself: "I make an agreement with myself to enjoy the best of life and to live the full wealth of my potential in harmony with nature and the universe." Follow the same sequence of moving the image up to the heart, to the frontal lobe, and out to the universe.

Follow these same steps in working with your spiritual body and higher self, saying: "I am at one with my God (Source) within and manifest its Glory." Continue the sequence of moving the image up to the heart, to the frontal lobe, and out to the universe.

The Yi Mind Power practice can also be very effective in helping us to solve problems. First, follow the initial steps outlined above, then:

1. Take the questions and problems that you have into your center of awareness (the lower Tan Tien/abdominal brain), then to your center of consciousness (the heart center/heart brain), then to your center of

observation (the mid-eyebrow/mind brain), then broadcast them out to the entire universe.

2. Wait for the answers and solutions to return to you clearly and distinctly. Allow them to ripen into full understanding. You can engage this practice at any time that you have questions or dilemmas or need to take action. Exhale your problem into the universe, open yourself, wait for a moment, and let go of the problem. You will become conscious of the solutions to your questions or problems. The more you practice this, the quicker and easier the results will come.

3. You must take action when you receive energy and information in response to the questions you have presented. The way to get extra energy for this action is by breathing red light into the heart three to six times, letting it radiate into the whole body through the heart. You will feel a lot of energy enabling you to take action and complete the task.

4. You can use the same technique to project your goals. Sometimes it helps to ask for more wisdom from the universe or cosmos in order to understand your life's purpose.

5. Finish the meditation by resting for a few moments and collecting the energy in your lower Tan Tien.

Planetary and Stellar Meditations to Increase Awareness and Sensitivity

Feeling the direct connection with the planetary energies is a unique experience that carries multiple benefits for yourself and for the healing practices you carry out for others. Practitioners of the Universal Tao meditations have noted the following benefits:

- An increase in emotional stability and in understanding the origin of emotional patterns.
- An ability to connect with information and energy from the universe.
- Strong healing processes in the organs and the whole body.
- A major increase in healing power.
- A greater balance between the weak and strong points of one's character.
- An increased ability to be deeply in touch with the different organs and systems in one's own body and in the people one treats.

Before proceeding with the planetary and stellar meditations we will explore in this chapter, prepare yourself by practicing some of the basic exercises for generating and directing Chi. These include: Iron Shirt Chi Kung, Inner Smile, Six Healing Sounds, Microcosmic Orbit, and One Finger Art. Next, practice Opening the Three Tan Tiens to the Six Directions. (See the first volume of *Taoist Cosmic Healing* for instruction in these practices.) Take some time to create a good contact with these energies and to integrate them into your body. Once the organs and energy centers are connected to the universal energy, the planetary forces can be integrated easily.

The planetary and stellar meditations are divided into seven parts. Each meditation represents a growing level of awareness and sensitivity. As is the case with all new practices and meditations, it takes some time to build up the connection, but with practice, it soon will become easier. As with anything in life, you will only get good at it if you master the basic principles and practice daily. If you want to go quickly in the beginning, you may have to return to the basics at a later stage. Once you really get it, you can choose to connect to the planetary and galactic energies at any moment during the day.

It is important to realize that in these meditations you are interacting with enormous forces. It is not the effort, but the awareness and resonance that determine the results. If you are open and receptive as you practice connecting with the planetary energies, you will find that you are affected by the energies at a level that you are able to handle. You may experience strong emotional, mental, and physical shifts in energy, but it will be manageable. However, if you try to manipulate the universe, you may suddenly be impacted by a lot more energy than you are prepared to deal with. You may soon discover that the ego has led you in this direction, and that you have "burned" yourself. Thus your energy level will decline instead of rise, with disappointment being the result.

A good way to familiarize yourself and get in contact with the planetary frequencies in the solar system (also known as "awareness belts") is to study some basic astronomy. The information and pictures in chapter 2, "Taoist Astrology and the Structure of the Universe," can help you gain a better understanding of how the solar system really appears. Simply look at the pictures and then close your eyes, look out through the cranium, and expand your awareness. It is important to respect the correct sequence of building up this meditation practice. Start with what you can clearly register with your senses. Begin with the sun (seeing the sun, sensing its warmth), then move to the earth (seeing it, feeling its gravity and energy), then shift to the moon (seeing the moon, feeling its coolness). You need to make contact with these three forces before you will be able to connect to the other planets. You do not have to see the planets in order to feel them; what we are getting in contact with is the energy/awareness belts of the planets. The planets in their materialized form are only the center of these belts.

Practice with great respect. Do not try to force these energies with your willpower. This will not work! Try to attract them. You can use the Eastern or Western astrological signs for the planets during the meditations by projecting them into the image of the planets, but it's better to start with only the color and quality of the planet.

To practice the following planetary meditations, complete each step before moving on to the next.

MEDITATION 1: EARTH-SUN-MOON TRIANGLE

1. Warm up with several basic exercises (Inner Smile, Cosmic Chi Kung, Tai Chi, Tao Yin, and others).
2. Practice Opening the Three Tan Tiens to the Six Directions.
3. Integrate the Inner Smile and the MCO (Microcosmic Orbit).
4. Connect to the Mother Earth force. Breathe deeply into the earth with every exhalation. Thank the earth for her love and nourishment. Breathe in the cool blue energy through the soles, the palms, and the perineum. Store this energy in your lower Tan Tien. This will be your safety belt and rooting during your planetary and galactic journey.
5. Bring your attention to the sacrum.
6. Picture a bright, full moon behind you, shining on your sacrum. The color of the moon can be seen and felt as silver-white.

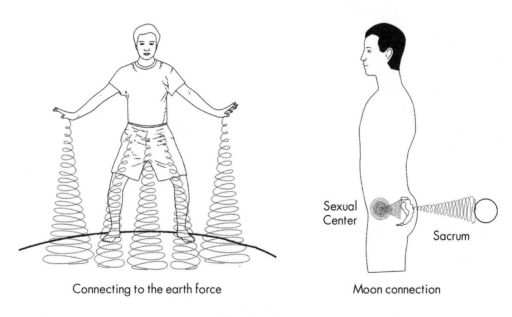

Connecting to the earth force

Moon connection

Sexual
Center

Sacrum

SEXUAL ENERGY

7. Breathe the moonlight into the sacrum, drawing it into the sexual center. The moonlight will be mixed inside the sexual center with the blue sexual energy. At the same time, draw the sexual energy inward. Men: pull up the sexual organ, perineum, and anus, and gently squeeze the

muscles around the prostate gland. Women: softly close and contract the vagina, perineum, and anus, and gently squeeze the muscles around the ovaries and the uterus. On the exhalation (men and women) release the muscles about 90 percent but keep the Chi inside. The squeezing should be very gentle, and the other muscles in the body should remain very relaxed. Gather the energy at the sexual center. Practice this for about five to ten minutes until you feel the moonlight directly entering into the sexual center.

8. Next, bring your attention to the third eye/mid-eyebrow point.

9. Picture a bright, gold/yellow sun in front of you. Feel the light particles and the cosmic Chi tingling on your face. Absorb this light in the third eye and the pituitary gland.

10. Breathe in the light and guide it from the third eye and the pituitary gland down into the heart.

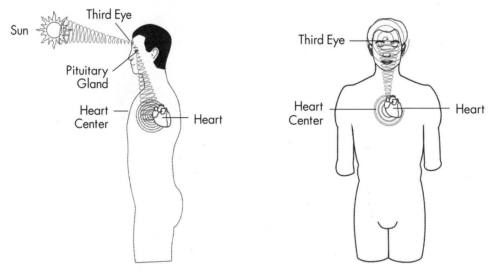

CONNECTING THE SUN WITH THE THIRD EYE AND HEART

11. Make the heart sound to clean the heart and balance the heart energy. Remember, from *Taoist Cosmic Healing*, that the healing sound of the heart is *Haww*. Feel love, peace, patience, and respect while you feel the sun directly shining in your heart. Shift your focus toward the heart center, right in the middle between the nipples and behind the sternum.

12. Blend the golden/yellow color of the sunlight with the bright red color of love and compassion in the heart center.

13. Gather more sunlight in the heart center. At a certain point the heart center will open up further and will connect with the force of universal love. A deep yet unsentimental love, which can be described as "the blooming of compassion" can be experienced.

14. On the inbreath draw the silver/white moonlight into the sacrum/sexual center (blue) and at the same time draw the golden/yellow sunlight into the third eye/heart center (red). On the outbreath condense these two energies in the central point behind the navel. (See illustrations below.) Push the blue/silver/white energy up and the red/golden/yellow energy down. Keep drawing these energies in until you feel a clear connection (ten to fifteen minutes).

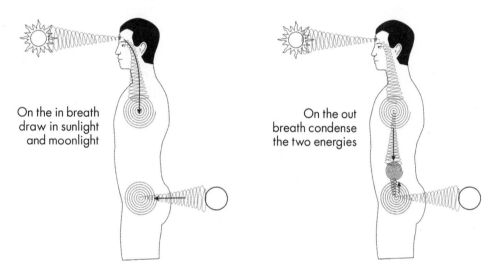

On the in breath draw in sunlight and moonlight

On the out breath condense the two energies

CONNECT THE SUN AND THE MOON

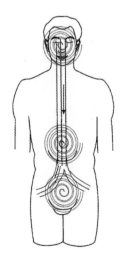

SUN AND MOON ENERGY IN THE BODY

15. Bring the kidney and sexual energy up through the vena cava and the heart energy down through the aorta.

16. Mix both energies in the lower Tan Tien. If you have difficulties working with the aorta and vena cava, just relax and let the two energies come together naturally in the lower Tan Tien.

17. When the love and sexual energy are combined in the sexual center, a soft orgasmic feeling will start vibrating in the lower Tan Tien, and from there through the whole body.

18. When the sun and moon energies are combined, their force is multiplied. Start slowly; do not take in too much sun and moonlight or you will begin to overheat. Give your body the time to adjust to the new energy level. If you feel that you are getting too hot, or if you have any adverse reactions or unpleasant sensations, practice the Six Healing Sounds (see *Taoist Cosmic Healing*) to cool down and regain equilibrium.

19. Next, move the energy from the lower Tan Tien down into the perineum and up into the Microcosmic Orbit (MCO).

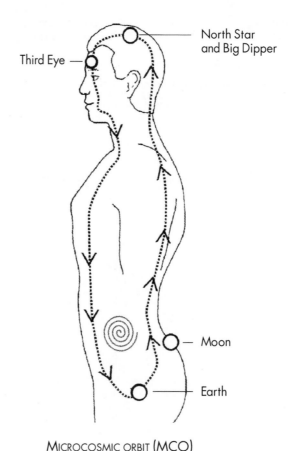

MICROCOSMIC ORBIT (MCO)

20. Put the emphasis on the following points and connections, stopping at each of these points to feel the external connection:
    Perineum—Earth
    Sacrum—Moon
    Crown—North Star/Big Dipper
    Third Eye—Sun
21. Circle the energy around the Microcosmic Orbit nine to eighteen times.
22. Then gather the energy in the lower Tan Tien and rest. Observe your body and energy in this resting state. Notice where the energy is moving in your body. Remain in this state for five to fifteen minutes.
23. End this meditation with Chi self-massage (see *Taoist Cosmic Healing*).

MEDITATION 2: STRENGTHENING THE ORGANS AND BALANCING THE EMOTIONS

1. Warm up with several basic exercises (Inner Smile, Cosmic Chi Kung, Tai Chi, Tao Yin, and others).
2. Practice Opening the Three Tan Tiens to the Six Directions.
3. Integrate the Inner Smile and the MCO (Microcosmic Orbit).
4. Make a firm, condensed Chi ball in the lower Tan Tien.
5. Connect to the Mother Earth force.
6. Bring your attention to the cranium and softly touch the cranial bones with a minimum of pressure. This touch is often called the "butterfly touch," as it is compared with the pressure you feel when a butterfly is landing on your hand. Next, connect to the craniosacral rhythm. Once you feel this rhythm, try to remain with it. Try it without hand contact. "Touch without touching"—holding your hand one to two centimeters from the skull.

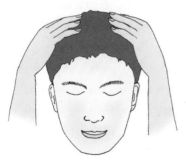

Base of the hand just above the ear

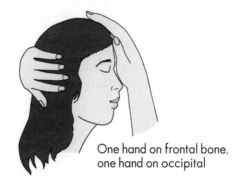

One hand on frontal bone, one hand on occipital

FEELING THE CRANIAL RHYTHM

7. Expand this cranial awareness to a distance of five to fifty centimeters away from the physical body. This will greatly increase the sensitivity in your skull and the craniosacral structure.

8. Make the connection between the organs, the cranium, and the related planets. Take a moment and connect your mind to your major organs, remembering the healing colors from *Taoist Cosmic Healing*. Next, bring your awareness to the head and let the awareness rise above to the planets. In time, this practice will blend into one sensation.

9. Put one hand (the "receiving hand," usually the nonpredominant one) on the spleen/pancreas area and fill these organs with the bright yellow light of openness, fairness, and trust. Put the second hand (the "giving hand," usually the predominant one) in the "beak position" softly on the crown point to make the internal connection with the sphenoid bone (see illustration opposite).

10. Hold this position and let the Chi move between the hands and between the sphenoid and the pancreas/spleen. Once you feel the connection, put the hands together in front of the lower Tan Tien. Then expand your cranial structure and look up with your eyes through your crown.

11. Visualize a bright yellow planet above you, the planet Saturn. Let the light of the planet Saturn shine down into the crown and the sphenoid bone and then directly down into the spleen and the pancreas. Feel the direct connection and feel how the spleen and pancreas are activated through this contact.

12. Feeling this connection may take some time, but once it has been established, the planets become like powerful batteries, charging your organs. Use this same procedure for the five main organs and planets, following the diagrams on pages 174 and 175.

13. Use an open hand on the other bones in the cranial system and not a "beak hand" as on the sphenoid bone. Use your giving hand on the cranium and your receiving one on the organs.

14. After you have finished working with the five main organs and planets in this way, picture all five planets above the crown and let their light shine into the five cranial entrances and further down into the organs. Then bring all these energies together in the the lower Tan Tien, forming a condensed Chi ball.

15. Next, move this energy through the Microcosmic Orbit, making nine to eighteen cycles.

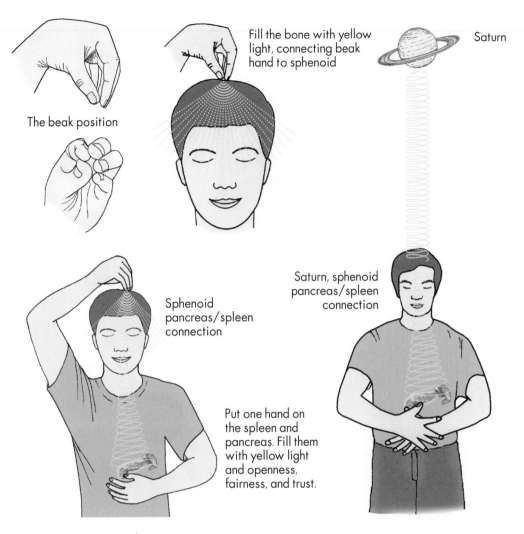

The beak position

Fill the bone with yellow light, connecting beak hand to sphenoid

Saturn

Sphenoid pancreas/spleen connection

Saturn, sphenoid pancreas/spleen connection

Put one hand on the spleen and pancreas. Fill them with yellow light and openness, fairness, and trust.

SPLEEN/PANCREAS, SPHENOID BONE, AND SATURN

16. Then gather the energy again in the lower Tan Tien and rest, receptively observing the body and the movement of energy.

17. End with Chi self-massage.

Note that during this meditation, you may meet different negative or undesirable emotions. Keep smiling down into the organs to enhance the virtue energy. If negative emotions keep bothering you, exhale them deeply into the earth and make the related healing sound. Fill the space with positive or virtue energy. (The virtue energies and healing sounds are discussed in detail in *Taoist Cosmic Healing*.)

One hand touches left parietal. Fill the bone with white light and courage.

Place the other hand just below the collarbone. Fill the lungs with white light and courage, righteousness. Connect left parietal and lung.

LUNGS, LEFT PARIETAL BONE, AND VENUS

Picture Venus as a white ball above the left parietal and connect them.

Venus

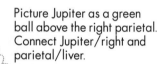

Put one hand on the liver. Fill the liver with green light and kindness.

The other hand touches the right parietal bone. Fill the bone with green light.

Connect liver and right parietal bone.

Jupiter

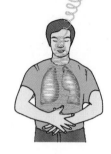

Picture Jupiter as a green ball above the right parietal. Connect Jupiter/right and parietal/liver.

LIVER, RIGHT PARIETAL BONE, AND JUPITER

Put one hand on the heart.
Fill the heart with red light,
love, peace, and respect.

The other hand touches the
frontal bone. Fill the frontal
bone with red light.

Connect the heart
and the frontal bone.

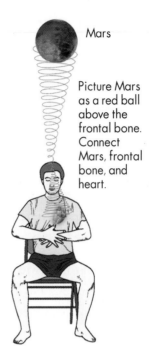

Mars

Picture Mars
as a red ball
above the
frontal bone.
Connect
Mars, frontal
bone, and
heart.

HEART, FRONTAL BONE, AND MARS

Put both hands on the kidneys.
Fill the kidneys with blue light
and gentleness.

One hand then
touches the
occipital bone.
Fill occipital
bone with
blue light.

The other hand touches Ming Men
(Door of Life at lumbar 2 and 3)
kidney point. Connect occipital
and kidneys.

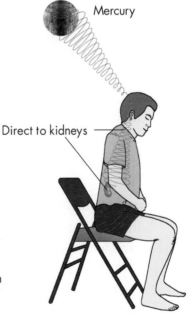

Mercury

Direct to kidneys

Picture Mercury as a blue
ball above the occipital.
Connect Mercury and
occipital.

KIDNEYS, OCCIPITAL BONE, AND MERCURY

Planetary
and Stellar
Meditations

MEDITATION 3: STRENGTHENING THE BODY SYSTEMS AND INCREASING THE ENERGY FIELD

After you have practiced the second meditation for a while it will become easier to feel the connection with the planetary forces. The third meditation uses the technique of the second meditation but adds two factors: the five earthly elemental forces and the expansion of the planet/organ energy into the body structures. This practice will strengthen the different organs and body systems. It will also create balance in your energy structures. Sickness and negative energy will be discharged, and your energy field will greatly improve.

1. Warm up with several basic exercises (Inner Smile, Cosmic Chi Kung, Tai Chi, Tao Yin, and others).
2. Practice Opening the Three Tan Tiens to the Six Directions.
3. Integrate the Inner Smile and the MCO (Microcosmic Orbit).
4. Make a firm, condensed Chi ball in the lower Tan Tien.
5. Connect to the Mother Earth force.
6. Go through the same five planets/organ cycle as in the second meditation, but now add the elemental force related to each organ: spleen-earth, lungs-metal, kidneys-water, liver-wood, heart-fire. Spend some time building up a connection with the different elemental forces.
7. Next, mix the elemental and planetary energies in the organs (see illustration opposite).
8. Then let the energy/color/virtue expand in the body systems until the whole body is filled and the energy radiates out into the aural field. Work with the organs/cranial bones/planets/elements/body systems in sequence outlined in the following steps.
9. Spleen/sphenoid bone/Saturn/earth element/muscular system. Earth energy can also be used in the lymphatic system.
10. Lungs/left parietal bone/Venus/metal element/breathing system.
11. Liver/right parietal bone/Jupiter/wood element/tendon and ligament system.
12. Heart/frontal bone/Mars/fire element/arterial and veinous system.
13. Kidneys/occipital bone/Mercury/water element/bone structure and hormonal system.

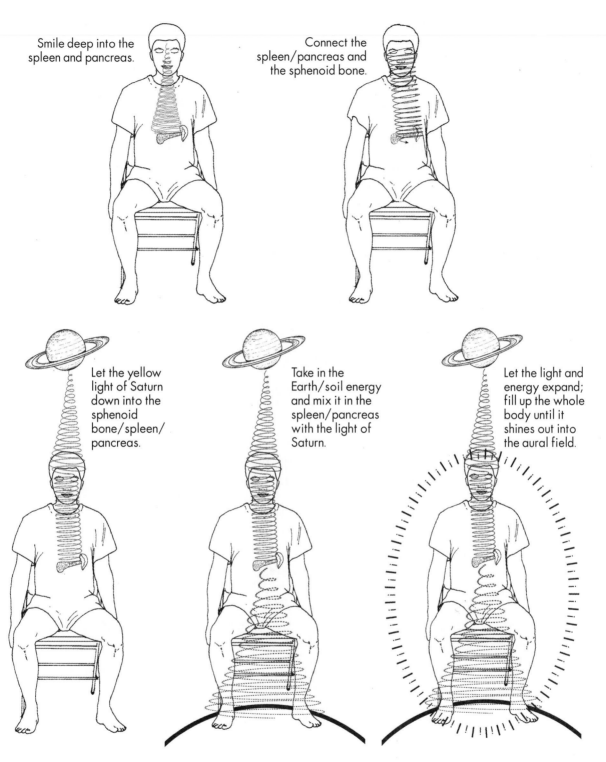

Smile deep into the spleen and pancreas.

Connect the spleen/pancreas and the sphenoid bone.

Let the yellow light of Saturn down into the sphenoid bone/spleen/pancreas.

Take in the Earth/soil energy and mix it in the spleen/pancreas with the light of Saturn.

Let the light and energy expand; fill up the whole body until it shines out into the aural field.

SPLEEN/SPHENOID BONE/SATURN/EARTH ELEMENT/MUSCULAR SYSTEM

Planetary and Stellar Meditations

After working with each organ/cranial bone/planet/element/body system, you will feel a strong, multicolored energy filling and surrounding your whole body.

14. Complete the meditation by adding the sun and moon energy. The sun is connected to the fire element, the pericardium, the third eye, and the lymph/immune system. The moon is connected to the water element, the sexual organs, the sacrum, and the hormonal system.

15. Envision all of the planets above and around you. Just relax and let the energy move freely throughout your body.

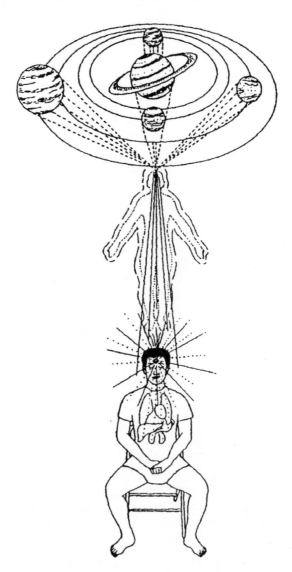

THE PLANETS' FORCES BEAM DOWN TO THE CRYSTAL ROOM

16. Gather the energy in the lower Tan Tien until you feel a Chi ball. Condense it firmly.

17. Cycle the Chi ball through the Microcosmic Orbit.

18. Then gather it again in the lower Tan Tien and rest, receptively observing for several minutes.

19. End with Chi self-massage.

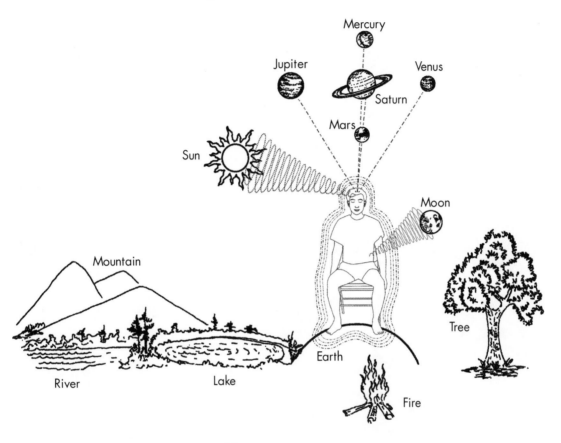

NATURAL FORCES

MEDITATION 4: CONNECTING TO THE STELLAR AND GALACTIC FORCES

Connecting with the stellar and galactic forces is a very strong form of meditation. It brings enormous amounts of energy into the body. The stellar and galactic meditation can be approached in two ways: the "six-direction method" and the "five-palace method." For either approach, always begin with the preparatory practices (explained in *Taoist Cosmic Healing*):

1. Warm up with several basic exercises (Inner Smile, Cosmic Chi Kung, Tai Chi, Tao Yin, and others).
2. Practice Opening the Three Tan Tiens to the Six Directions.
3. Integrate the Inner Smile and the MCO (Microcosmic Orbit).
4. Make a firm, condensed Chi ball in the lower Tan Tien.
5. Connect to the Mother Earth force.

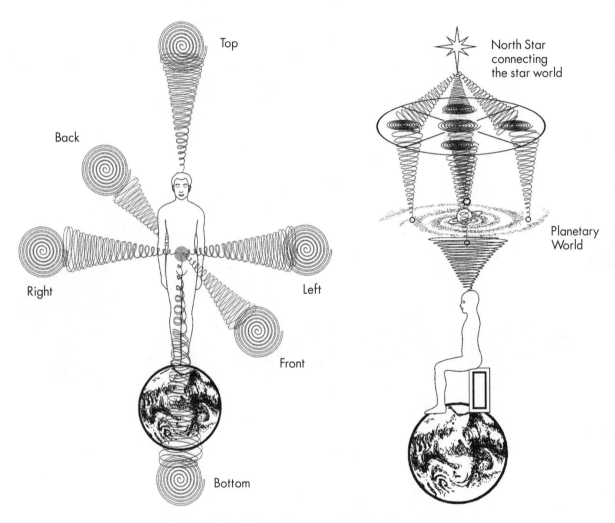

GALAXY CONNECTION IN THE SIX DIRECTIONS AND
GALAXY CONNECTION WITH THE FIVE PALACES

In the six-direction method, golden yellow is the color used most frequently, but any other colors can be incorporated as they manifest. The entrance points are the crown, the third eye, the navel, the door of life/Ming Men point, and the feet. This meditation will balance the energy throughout the body since the connection points are in the head, body, and legs. The bottom galaxy is reached through the earth, which means that good grounding is easy. This takes away the risk of overheating. Always remember that galactic energy is enormously powerful; maintain a respectful attitude as you work with these energies. (Universal Tao's instructional video *Cosmic Healing Chi Kung: Six Directions Channeling* provides a thorough explanation of this practice.)

In the five-palace method, the energy is brought into the body through the cranium, so there needs to be a good rooting and connection with the earth to balance the powerful, hot, universal energy coming in through the head. Meditation 1, "Earth-Sun-Moon Triangle" can be practiced first. It is advisable to begin with planetary connections and meditations, as the energy and heat these practices generate is lower than that of the galaxies. Once the planetary energies are balanced in the head, expand the awareness further, beyond the Milky Way and into the galactic world. Connect with the North Star and build up the connection with the five palaces around the North Star.

Next, use the corresponding colors, organs, planets, elements, and cranial bones (see opposite page). Bring the energy all the way down to the five organs.

Once you have mastered this meditation you can increase the energy level by connecting the seven stars of the Big Dipper with the bones of the skull. See illustrations, below and on page 182.

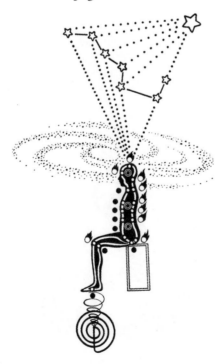

NORTH STAR AND BIG DIPPER CONNECTING WITH THE HUMAN BODY

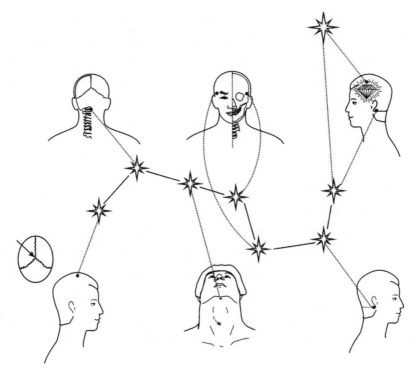

NORTH STAR AND BIG DIPPER CONNECTING WITH POINTS OF THE SKULL

IMMORTAL CONNECTING TO THE GALACTIC FORCES

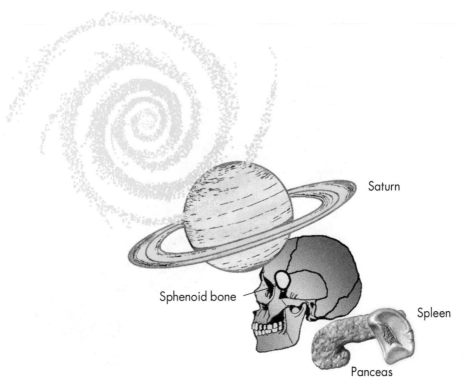

Saturn

Sphenoid bone

Spleen

Panceas

CENTRAL PALACE—YELLOW GALAXY

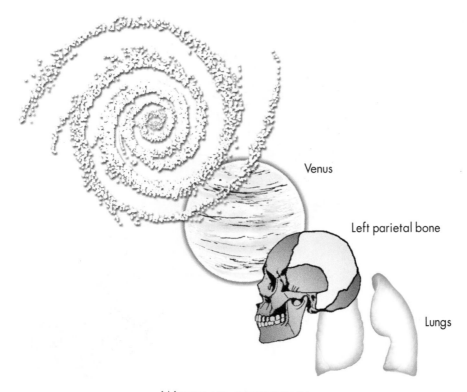

Venus

Left parietal bone

Lungs

WEST PALACE—WHITE GALAXY

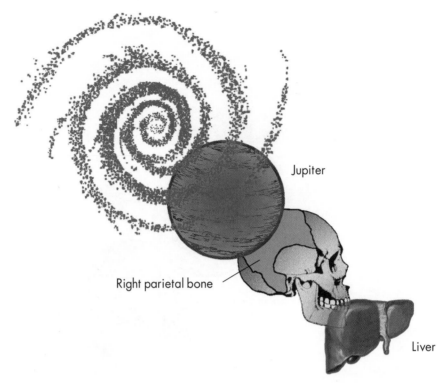

EAST PALACE—GREEN GALAXY

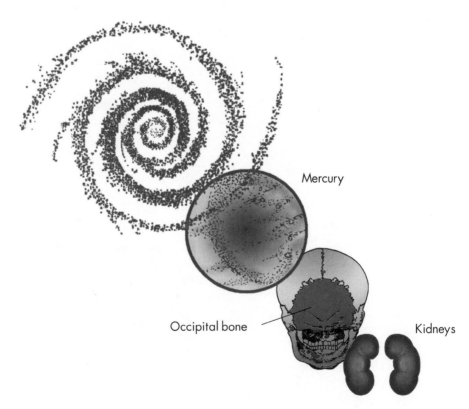

NORTH PALACE—BLUE GALAXY

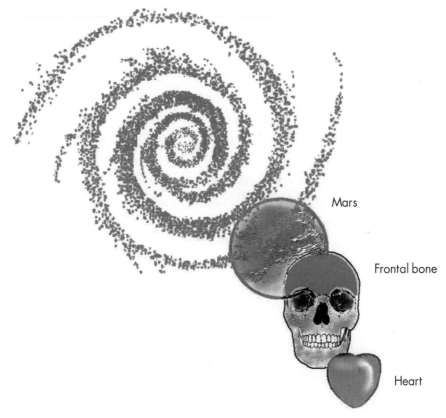

Mars

Frontal bone

Heart

SOUTHERN PALACE—RED GALAXY

MEDITATION 5: BALANCING THE PLANETARY AND STELLAR INFLUENCES

Regular practice of the first four meditations will reveal to you which of the five elements is your strongest influence and which is your weakest. There are different ways you may discover this. For example, you may realize that you have a weak connection with one of the elements because you experience emotions, pain, and tension during the meditation, or you might notice an inability to sense its corresponding color, organ, or planetary influence.

After practicing the first four meditations for some time, you will probably notice that you:

1. Are able to feel the connection between the corresponding planetary and galactic/palace frequencies;
2. Are able to feel the connection between the corresponding cranial bones and organs;
3. Are able expand the energies into the related body systems.

One system of linked planets/star palaces/cranial bones/organs/elements/body systems will probably be very easy to feel, while another system may seem absent. This difference is due to unconscious physical, emotional, and mental imbalances. It is also possible that you may feel a particular planetary energy but not its corresponding star palace, or the other way around. Be as sensitive and clear as possible about the different energies and connections you experience, as this can provide a lot of information about your personality and soul. Once you have discovered particular imbalances and how they are anchored in your system, you can use this information during meditation as a tool to improve weaknesses in your personality and physical body. A sensitivity to your body, its emotional patterns, and its energy systems will develop over time. In the beginning, we do a lot of "practice" to become people who are ultimately self-aware at all times. We then come to experience a natural state of thinking and being in which negative issues become merely something to transform; we see them as temporary issues, not a permanent situation.

The fifth planetary/stellar meditation, which uses the five-palace method illustrated on page 180, employs the principle of "full" and "empty" functions in the body. This principle is one of the most fundamental in oriental medicine. The cause of health problems essentially lies in a *lack* of energy and information in one part of the energy system that corresponds to an *overactivity* in other parts. One example of this imbalance can be seen in the way many people rely almost exclusively on particular, well-developed skills and personality characteristic to the exclusion of other abilities and traits, which are poorly developed. These imbalances may be informed by the individual's karmic imprints or may arise from present life choices.

Work with linking the energies of the star palaces, planets, cranial bones, organs, elemental forces, and body systems as you have with the preceding meditations, but focus on the energy systems with which you have the strongest and weakest connection. The principle of this meditation is that you use the excess energy from the overactive system to nurture the deficient system. As an example, let's say you feel a strong connection with the green galaxy/Jupiter/right parietal bone/liver, but feel a weak connection with the white galaxy/Venus/left parietal bone/lungs. This might also show up in liver overactivity and lung weakness. You might notice a tendency to irritation, anger, and control as well as depression and discouragement. Use the strong connection you have with the green galaxy/Jupiter/right parietal bone/liver system to strengthen your connection with, and direct additional energy into, the white galaxy/Venus/left parietal bone/lungs system. In this way, you direct more vitality into the weak organ, and often information and insight about balancing your personality characteristics arises spontaneously.

1. Warm up with several basic exercises (Inner Smile, Cosmic Chi Kung, Tai Chi, Tao Yin, and others).
2. Practice Opening the Three Tan Tiens to the Six Directions.
3. Integrate the Inner Smile and the MCO (Microcosmic Orbit).
4. Make a firm, condensed Chi ball in the lower Tan Tien.
5. Connect to the Mother Earth force.
6. Begin the process of making the connection between the corresponding organs, cranial bones, planets, galaxies, and elemental forces, as outlined in the previous meditations. However, work first with the strongest system, in this case, the green galaxy/Jupiter/right parietal bone/liver system. Fill the body with the related color (green).
7. Next, change the color in the body and aural field to the color related to the weakest system, in this case the white galaxy/Venus/left parietal bone/lungs system (white). Draw this color inside the lungs. Put both hands on the lungs until you feel the energy tingling inside the organs.
8. Put one hand on the left parietal bone and feel the lung/left parietal connection.
9. Once you feel this connection, put your hands together in front of the navel and turn your eyes to the left, upward, and inward, looking into and through the left parietal bone and then outside of the skull in the direction of Venus and the white galaxy.
10. Visualize a clear white ball above you. At a certain point, the energy of Venus will shine down directly into the body. Keep your attention focused and expand your awareness through Venus toward the white galaxy.

    Do this transition from the strongest to the weakest system, using the related colors, several times until the energy feels more balanced. If the transition does not work, let the color of the strongest system (in this case, green) expand and project through the weakest system (in this case, the left parietal bone/Venus/white galaxy) until you feel the color of the weakest system clearly (in this case, white). Let the white light shine on your skull and fill up the whole body and aura. Feel both the strongest and the weakest systems, and balance their energies further into the body and the aural field.

11. To increase the effect, expand the energy into the respiratory system. Breathe through the skin of your whole body.
12. Now, gather the energy in the lower Tan Tien, making a condensed Chi ball.
13. Circulate it through the Microcosmic Orbit.
14. Then gather it again in the lower Tan Tien, and rest.
15. End with Chi self-massage.

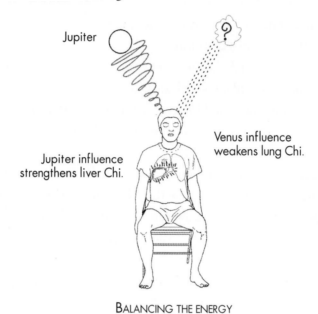

Jupiter

Jupiter influence
strengthens liver Chi.

Venus influence
weakens lung Chi.

BALANCING THE ENERGY

MEDITATION 6: BALANCING THE YIN/YANG EXTREMES IN THE STAR WORLD

The star world is so immense that it is difficult for the undeveloped human mind to grasp. It is part of the materialized universe, and in this way it is part of the world of polarity and yin and yang.

Many scientists believe that a black hole is the evolutionary end-point of a massive star that has collapsed to a point of zero volume and infinite density, creating what is known as a "singularity," from which matter and even light cannot escape. Yet according to Taoist belief, in the material world, infinite density cannot exist. Infinity cannot be found within the materialized sphere. Black holes are indeed points of extreme density, but only to the point that extreme yin turns into its opposite. Extreme darkness starts to produce light again. Many contemporary Taoist astrologers believe that, although it is not yet measurable, light particles do escape from black holes.

Quasars are thought to be the very bright centers of certain distant galax-

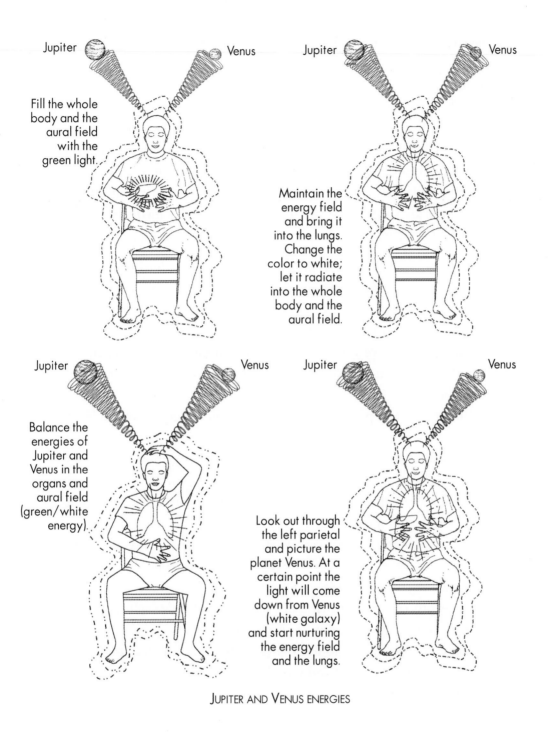

Fill the whole body and the aural field with the green light.

Maintain the energy field and bring it into the lungs. Change the color to white; let it radiate into the whole body and the aural field.

Balance the energies of Jupiter and Venus in the organs and aural field (green/white energy).

Look out through the left parietal and picture the planet Venus. At a certain point the light will come down from Venus (white galaxy) and start nurturing the energy field and the lungs.

Jupiter and Venus energies

ies in which some sort of energetic action is occurring, probably due to the presence of a supermassive black hole in the same galaxy. From the perspective of Taoist astrology, quasars are points of extreme light where extreme yang turns into its opposite.

Black holes and quasars are the yin and yang extremes of the star world.

Planetary
and Stellar
Meditations

In the sixth meditation we will use these two poles to project our awareness beyond the world of phenomena.

Before proceeding with this meditation, it is important that you have taken sufficient time to master the first five meditations. Only then can this advanced meditation serve your spiritual development. If you are not prepared, it can be harmful. We advise that you contact an experienced Universal Tao Cosmic Healing instructor to introduce you to this level of practice. If you suffer regular headaches, heart problems, or mental or emotional problems, we strongly suggest that you do not undertake this meditation.

The following are the principles of this meditation:

1. Start with the warm up and preparation exercises outlined with each of the preceding meditations. It is very important to establish a good centering/grounding.
2. Expand your awareness into the star world.
3. Connect high above you with the North Star and the Big Dipper.
4. Let the light from the North Star and the Big Dipper fill your upper Tan Tien.
5. Connect with two points that you visualize on either side of the North Star. One point is an extreme light/yang point (quasar). The other point is an extreme dark/yin point (black hole). (See illustration opposite.)
6. Visualize these two points circling around the North Star.
7. Let the process speed up and continue automatically while your attention goes in and through the North Star.
8. At a certain point, the process will speed up so much that you will start to feel a lifting sensation, and the edge or boundary between yin and yang will start to fade away.
9. Let this process continue naturally, until yin and yang melt together. At this point, pure yang or ultimate yang energy arises.
10. Always remember to go to the Wu Chi, the place of nothingness, at the end of a meditation. Rest and give the "practice" time to do the work it was intended to do.

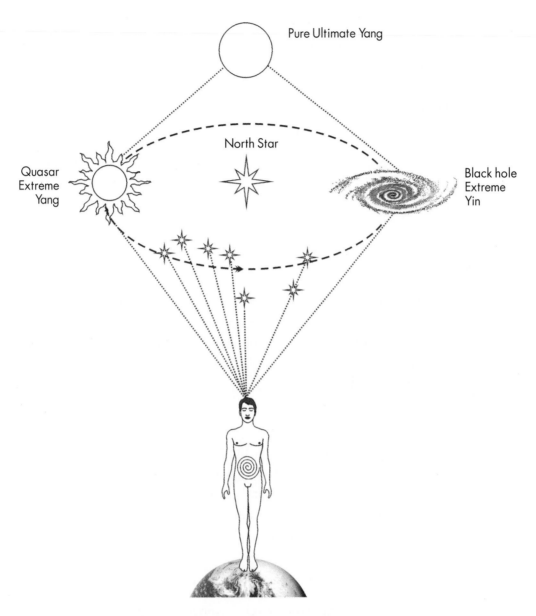

CONNECTING WITH QUASAR AND BLACK HOLE

MEDITATION 7: YIN STAGE AWARENESS PRACTICE

In this meditation the intention is to let the planetary and galactic forces enter the body spontaneously. During this practice, do not use willpower, intention, or effort to attract the energies of any particular planet or star palace; rather, allow yourself to just be open and receptive to the planetary and galactic forces. Planetary and galactic forces are influencing us every second of our lives. The only choice we have is whether or not to be aware of it—the influence is there anyway. Our dominant planetary and galactic influences change many times in a day. When we sit still and empty the mind we can observe the subtle process of shifts in planetary and galactic energies, as well as shifts in the energy fields in our cranium, organs, and body systems.

During a yin-stage, or passive, meditation you can observe energy from different dimensions of the universe:

- nature energies, including trees, lakes, mountains, thunder, lightning, wind, and so forth;
- planets;
- individual stars;
- galaxies, quasars, pulsars, black holes;
- elemental forces

When you learn to observe this process you will be able to feel the direct influence of the planets and stars in that particular moment. It will give you the freedom to understand specific universal influences and how they affect your physical and energetic condition and your emotional and thinking processes. It also will provide insight and information that can clarify tensions or dynamics in your relationships.

The yin-stage awareness meditation works very well in groups. Many different processes will be occurring at the same time. As the group meditates together, the planetary and stellar energies will work on each individual, on dynamics between the individuals, and on the collective energy of the group as a whole. Experience has shown that even in large group meditations, 50–80 percent of the participants experience the same planetary and galactic forces entering their energetic fields.

To practice this meditation (alone or with a group), follow these steps:

1. Warm up with several basic exercises (Inner Smile, Cosmic Chi Kung, Tai Chi, Tao Yin, and others).
2. Practice Opening the Three Tan Tiens to the Six Directions.
3. Integrate the Inner Smile and the MCO (Microcosmic Orbit).
4. Make a firm, condensed Chi ball in the lower Tan Tien.
5. Connect to the Mother Earth force.
6. Bring your attention to the cranium, feel the cranial rhythm, and expand the cranial rhythm into the aural field.
7. If you are meditating with a group, connect to the energy field of the others.

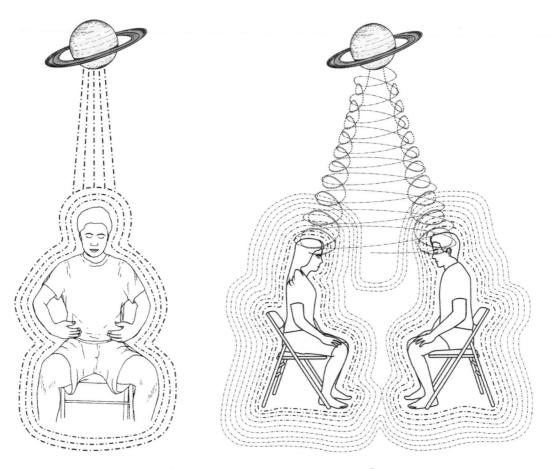

INDIVIDUAL AND 2-PERSON AWARENESS MEDITATION WITH SATURN INFLUENCE

8. Then, just relax, be receptive, and observe what happens. If you wish, you can softly say to the others what you feel happening in your body or cranium.

9. At the end of the meditation session, draw the energy back into your own individual field.

10. Gather the energy into the lower Tan Tien and make a condensed Chi ball.

11. Circulate the energy throughout the MCO.

12. Then gather the energy again in the lower Tan Tien, and rest.

13. End with Chi self-massage.

First, practice individually, or, if you practice in a group, stay with your individual experience. After a while you will be able to distinguish your personal energy field from the shared or group energy field. If you have difficulty feeling these energies, meditate with someone who has a better connection

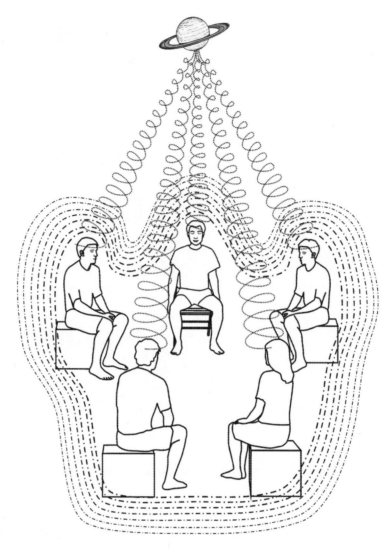

GROUP AWARENESS MEDITATION WITH SATURN INFLUENCE

with the planets, but stay with your own experience. Be patient and relax. You can be sure that the planetary and stellar energies are there, it just takes some time and practice to become sensitive to them.

Using Taoist Astral Healing to Help Others

The therapeutic potential of the meditation practices described throughout this book is unlimited. The planetary and stellar energies can be used with great success in self-healing, but it is also very easy to integrate them into healing and bodywork practices for the benefit of others. This chapter discusses some basic principles for using Taoist Cosmic Healing techniques in healing treatments.

It can be very powerful to combine the meditation practices of Taoist Cosmic Healing with Chi Nei Tsang (internal organ Chi massage). (See Universal Tao Publications' *Chi Nei Tsang*, vols. I and II, for more information.) Both methods seek to balance the energies in the body and to activate the life force. Chi Nei Tsang uses the lower Tan Tien as the main area of diagnosis and treatment. Imbalances in energy and tension in the lower Tan Tien are treated with a firm physical pressure and with the three forces of the universe (earth, cosmic, and universal) as the nurturing source. In Taoist Cosmic Healing the emphasis is on connecting the body with the five elemental forces, the planets, and the stars, often without touching the body.

Chi Nei Tsang works mainly from the lower Tan Tien toward the universe (from material energy to subtle energy), while Cosmic Healing works from the universe toward the lower Tan Tien (from subtle energy to material energy). The combination of these two systems will give you the ability to integrate internal and external energy in the lower Tan Tien.

In practicing the Universal Tao system, it is important to stay clear and grounded. The purpose of planetary and galactic healing is to reconnect ourselves and our students with the energy of nature, planets, stars, and the

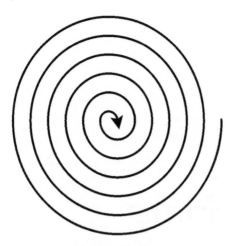

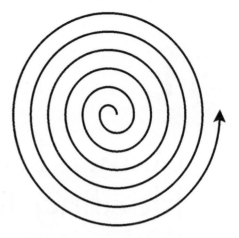

Cosmic Healing: Starting from the universal laws and integrating them into the physical body.

Chi Nei Tsang: Starting from the lower Tan Tien and connecting with the universal laws. From matter into subtle energy.

TAOIST COSMIC HEALING AND CHI NEI TSANG

Cosmic Healing

External Universe

Lower Tan Tien

Internal Universe

Chi Nei Tsang

External Universe

EXTERNAL AND INTERNAL UNIVERSES

higher universal frequencies. While spectacular healing experiences may occur, we should remember that there are no shortcuts on the spiritual path. The Taoist Cosmic Healing practices are very effective in:

• activating the life force in the body, which triggers self-healing;
• releasing and transforming blocked and negative energy;
• creating a strong spiritual connection and a higher awareness level.

Although the practices discussed in this book are easy to learn for anyone with enough interest and perseverance, the effectiveness of a healing treatment depends on the healing practitioner's level of energy, connection with elemental and universal forces, and ability to perceive the student/patient's needs. These abilities can only be cultivated by practicing the Taoist Cosmic Healing meditations on a regular basis and fully integrating them into your daily life.

GENERAL HEALING SESSION

The following healing session describes a practice involving only one student, however this practice can also be performed with a group. Before starting this healing session, you and the student should warm up with several basic meditation exercises.

There are two ways to approach this type of healing session. One way is to focus on the energies in your own body, modeling the steps you would like the student to perform, while asking him or her to follow along, focusing on the energies in his or her body. In this way, you go through the complete healing procedure together. Another way is to work together with the student(s) to create a collective energy body between and above you that links your energy fields. You then focus on the energy body together while you practice each step of the meditation.

1. Sit across from the student. Together, warm up with several basic exercises.
2. Make a firm, condensed Chi ball in the lower Tan Tien.
3. Connect to the mother Earth force.
4. Create a Chi field, as described in chapter 9. Gradually feel that the room has become charged with universal Chi.
5. If you are going to work with an energy body, link your personal star with the student's personal star. Link the personal stars to an energy body above you. (See chapter 9.)

6. Focus on the lower Tan Tien and connect to the universe.

7. Be aware of your sacrum area and feel the Chi. Transfer this energy up to the crown and out to the universe. Then spiral the Chi back down to the energy body and it will go down to the student's physical body.

8. Draw green light in from the universe with your palm and push the green light through the sacrum to push the sickness/blocked energy out to the other side of the universe. Repeat this procedure—pulling green light from the universe and pushing the sick energy out into the universe—six to nine times, until you feel the sacrum is clean.

9. Visualize the sacrum and vitalize the complete bone structure with yellow light, which will help strengthen the sacrum bone.

10. Be aware of the energy body above you. Extend your awareness above your crown, and channel white light down from the center of the galaxy and violet light from the North Pole.

11. Using your mind power, invite the inside of the sacrum bone in the energy body to open, allowing the white and violet light to flow into the marrow. Focus on the energy body; picture the energy body's sacrum and bone structure. Guide the energy inside, and see the whole body light up from deep inside.

12. Next, focus on the adrenal-kidney/Ming Men point and the navel. Flush them with green light to clean them out.

13. Now, draw yellow light in from the universe through the Ming Men to the navel and then back out to the universe. To cool down the Ming Men (if necessary), draw blue light from a blue pool of water in the center of a spiraling galaxy in the universe in through the navel to the Ming Men and then back out to the universe.

14. Then bring white or violet light down and activate the lower Tan Tien. Explain to your student that the lower Tan Tien is like an ocean and the body is like a hollow bamboo. The bamboo can draw on the boundless supply of water, and the energy will never dry up.

15. Concentrate on the solar plexus and T-11 (the point opposite the solar plexus). Draw green light in through the T-11 point, spiral it through the solar plexus, then flush the green light out into the universe. Next, energize the solar plexus with white and violet light. Always allow the energy to stream through both points fully, allowing plenty of time and energy to do the intended job.

16. When working with the solar plexus, which holds the emotions, the most important thing to remember is to connect the backside of the

solar plexus to the universe. There is literally no end to this connection. Allow the Chi to come all the way down, and allow any images to form and be released. Then stabilize the energy. The mental images that may form in the mind of the person you are treating may be disturbing or evoke sadness; disturbing memories tend to get stuck in the solar plexus and cause energy blockages. The release of these images produces an emotional release. The individual being treated may laugh or cry, so be sure to stay emotionally neutral to allow a safe space for this special kind of release.

17. Picture the Chi field encompassing the student as a big protective bubble. Cool down with blue light that you draw from a cool pool in the universe.

18. Proceed to the heart and the point on the vertebrae immediately opposite the heart. Draw green light in from the universe and draw it through the two areas, as before. Repeat this several times.

19. Now scan the student's heart with your palm, judging its strength. Next select the strength of the red color to use in the healing practice (from pink to deep crimson, but never too dark). We use red to strengthen the heart, but make sure there's no infection in the body. It is best to energize the heart with white that has strands of red light. Send red light through the heart, strengthening it.

20. Cool down any excess heat in the heart, drawing blue light into the heart and flushing it out through the spinal area opposite the heart. Next, draw white light into the heart and push it out in the same way.

21. Energize the center at the back of the heart using violet and golden Chi. Picture the heart surrounded by a golden aura.

22. Move up to the throat center and flush it with green light through C-7, the seventh cervical vertebra. Next draw blue light in from the universe and push it through, as before. The throat center responds very well to blue light; it opens and clears it.

23. Next, activate the mid-eyebrow. Focus on the mideyebrow in your own body. Draw in golden yellow light and use it to flush and stabilize the area. Flush it all the way through to the back of the head. Then energize the mid-eyebrow with violet and golden light.

24. Finally, concentrate on the crown. Draw violet and golden light into the crown, and then direct the light all the way down through the center channel, flushing the entire channel and leaving the body at the perineum.

25. Cool down the system by showering blue light over the whole body.
26. Finish your healing session by standing in front of the person you are treating with your hands in a prayer position. Focus your mind on the North Star and bring the luminous violet light mixed with white light from the universe down into the energy body above you. Let the colors wash through the energy body, into the personal stars, then into yourself and the person you are treating, thus energizing everyone involved. All the participants should then rest in the yin stage/awareness meditation. Clear the mind and let the practice session do the healing work it was intended to do.

Bibliography

Blechschmidt, E., and R. F. Gasser. *Biokinetics and Biodynamics of Human Differentiation*. Springfield, Ill.: Thomas Books, 1978.

Carus, Paul. *Chinese Astrology*. Malaysia: Pelanduk Publications, 1992.

Chia, Mantak. *Awakening Healing Light*. Huntington, N.Y.: Universal Tao Publications, 1993.

———. *Chi Nei Tsang*. Huntington, N.Y.: Universal Tao Publications, 1990.

———. *Fusion of the Five Elements I*. Huntington, N.Y.: Universal Tao Publications, 1989.

———. *Healing Love through the Tao*. Huntington, N.Y.: Universal Tao Publications, 1986.

———. *Iron Shirt Chi Kung*. Huntington, N.Y.: Universal Tao Publications, 1986.

———. *Taoist Cosmic Healing*. Rochester, Vt.: Destiny Books, 2003.

———. *Taoist Secrets of Love: Cultivating Male Sexual Energy*. New York: Aurora Press, 1984.

Gerber, Richard. *Vibrational Medicine*. Santa Fe: Bear & Company, 1988.

Kushi, Michio. *One Peaceful World*. New York: St .Martin's Press, 1987.

———. *Other Dimensions: Exploring the Unexplained*. New York: Avery Penguin Putnam, 1991.

———. *The Teachings of Michio Kushi*. Becket, Mass.: One Peaceful World Press, 1993.

Liang, Shou-Yu, Yang and Wu. *Baguazhang (Emei Baguazhang)*. Jamaica Plain, Mass.: YMAA Publication Center, 1994.

Mann, A. T. *The Round Art: The Astrology of Time and Space*. Limpsfield, Eng.: Paper Tiger, 1979.

Masunaga, Shizuto. *Zen Shiatsu*. Tokyo: Japan Publications, 1979.

Matsumato, Kiiko, and Stephen Birch. *Hara Diagnosis: Reflection on the Sea, Stems, and Branches*. Brookline, Mass.: Paradigm Publications, 1998.

Milne, Hugh. *The Heart of Listening*. Berkeley: North Atlantic Books, 1995.

Ni, Hua Ching. *The Book of Changes and the Unchanging Truth*. Malibu, Calif.: Shrine of the Eternal Breath of Tao, 1983.

———. *Taoist Inner View of the Universe and the Immortal Realm*. Malibu, Calif.: Shrine of the Eternal Breath of Tao, 1979.

Nicolson, Iain, and Patrick Moore. *The Universe*. Oxford: Equinox, 1985.

Sadler, Thomas. *Langman's Medical Embryology*. Baltimore: Williams and Wilkins Company, 1966.

Upledger, John. *Craniosacral Therapy*. Seattle: Eastland Press, 1983.

Veltman. *Mensen en Planeten*. Netherlands: Christofoor Zeist, 1993.

Walter, Derek. *Chinese Astrology*. London: Aquarian Press, 1987.

———. *The Chinese Astrology Workbook*. London: Aquarian Press, 1988.

West, John. *The Serpent in the Sky: The High Wisdom of Ancient Egypt*. Wheaton, Ill.: Quest Books, 1993.

About the Authors

MANTAK CHIA

Mantak Chia has been studying the Taoist approach to life since childhood. His mastery of this ancient knowledge, enhanced by his study of other disciplines, has resulted in the development of the Universal Tao System, which is now taught throughout the world.

Mantak Chia was born in Thailand to Chinese parents in 1944. When he was six years old, he learned from Buddhist monks how to sit and "still the mind." While in grammar school, he learned traditional Thai boxing, and soon went on to acquire considerable skill in Aikido, Yoga, and Tai Chi. His studies of the Taoist way of life began in earnest when he was a student in Hong Kong, ultimately leading to his mastery of a wide variety of esoteric disciplines. To better understand the mechanisms behind healing energy, he also studied Western anatomy and medical sciences.

Master Chia has taught his system of healing and energizing practices to tens of thousands of students and trained more than two thousand instructors and practitioners throughout the world. He has established centers for Taoist study and training in many countries around the globe. In June 1990 he was honored by the International Congress of Chinese Medicine and Qigong (Chi Kung), which named him the Qigong Master of the Year.

DIRK OELLIBRANDT

Dirk Oellibrandt has been practicing various forms of martial arts since the age of thirteen. After many years of training, he has become adept at Chi Kung, Tai Chi, Aikido, and the *Pa kua* Practices. He also learned to work with energy in a healing capacity, and studied shiatsu, oriental medicine, and osteopathy. Dirk and his wife, Katrien, direct the Du Mai Clinic in Belgium, which explores the dynamics between universal laws and the re-creation of the human body through a diverse range of healing traditions.

The Universal Tao System and Training Center

THE UNIVERSAL TAO SYSTEM

The ultimate goal of Taoist practice is to transcend physical boundaries through the development of the soul and the spirit within the human. That is also the guiding principle behind the Universal Tao, a practical system of self-development that enables individuals to complete the harmonious evolution of their physical, mental, and spiritual bodies. Through a series of ancient Chinese meditative and internal energy exercises, the practitioner learns to increase physical energy, release tension, improve health, practice self-defense, and gain the ability to heal him- or herself and others. In the process of creating a solid foundation of health and well-being in the physical body, the practitioner also creates the basis for developing his or her spiritual potential by learning to tap into the natural energies of the sun, moon, earth, stars, and other environmental forces.

The Universal Tao practices are derived from ancient techniques rooted in the processes of nature. They have been gathered and integrated into a coherent, accessible system for well-being that works directly with the life force, or Chi, that flows through the meridian system of the body.

Master Chia has spent years developing and perfecting techniques for teaching these traditional practices to students around the world through ongoing classes, workshops, private instruction, and healing sessions, as well as books and video and audio products. Further information can be obtained at www.universal-tao.com.

UNIVERSAL TAO TRAINING CENTER

The Tao Garden Resort and Training Center in northern Thailand is the home of Master Chia and serves as the worldwide headquarters for Universal

Tao activities. This integrated wellness, holistic health, and training center is situated on eighty acres surrounded by the beautiful Himalayan foothills near the historic walled city of Chiang Mai. The serene setting includes flower and herb gardens ideal for meditation, open-air pavilions for practicing Chi Kung, and a health and fitness spa.

The Center offers classes year-round, as well as summer and winter retreats. It can accommodate two hundred students, and group leasing can be arranged. For more information, you may fax the Center at (66)(53) 495-852, or email universaltao@universal-tao.com.

Index

BOOKS OF RELATED INTEREST

TAOIST COSMIC HEALING
Chi Kung Color Healing Principles for
Detoxification and Rejuvenation
by Mantak Chia

SEXUAL REFLEXOLOGY
Activating the Taoist Points of Love
by Mantak Chia and Willlam U. Wei

THE WARRIOR AS HEALER
A Martial Arts Herbal for Power, Fitness, and Focus
by Thomas Richard Joiner

NEI KUNG
The Secret Teachings of the Warrior Sages
by Kosta Danaos

QIGONG TEACHINGS OF A TAOIST IMMORTAL
The Eight Essential Exercises of Master Li Ching-yun
by Stuart Alve Olson

T'AI CHI ACCORDING TO THE I CHING
Embodying the Principles of the Book of Changes
by Stuart Alve Olson

THE COMPLETE I CHING
The Definitive Translation
by the Taoist Master Alfred Huang

MARTIAL ARTS TEACHING TALES OF POWER AND PARADOX
Freeing the Mind, Focusing Chi, and Mastering the Self
by Pascal Fauliot

Inner Traditions • Bear & Company
P.O. Box 388
Rochester, VT 05767
1-800-246-8648
www.InnerTraditions.com

Or contact your local bookseller